CONNECTICUT HABEAS CORPUS

REPRESENTING PETITIONERS

Attorney Michael Fitzpatrick

Attorney Jay Ruane

Attorney Jim Ruane

AUTHOR'S NOTE

This publication is intended to serve as resource and guide for attorneys and petitioners in Connecticut habeas corpus cases. It does not cover every permutation of Connecticut habeas corpus jurisprudence, which is a vast body of law. Nor does it cover federal habeas corpus practice and procedure. Practitioners should also monitor the law for new developments. For further information and assistance, contact Ruane Attorneys at 203-925-9200. We can discuss your situation during a consultation.

TABLE OF CONTENTS

CHAPTER 1:
HABEAS CORPUS JURISPRUDENCE

A. Overview

"[A] fundamental value determination of our society [is] that it is far worse to convict an innocent man than to let a guilty man go free."

In re Winship, 397 U.S. 374, 372 (1970)

"Today, as in prior centuries, the writ [of habeas corpus] is a bulwark against convictions that violate 'fundamental fairness.'"

Engle v. Isaac, 456 U.S. 107, 126 (1982)

The right to habeas corpus is guaranteed by the federal and state constitutions. Article I, § 9 of the United States Constitution provides that "[t]he Privilege of the Writ of

Habeas Corpus shall not be suspended, unless when in Cases or Rebellion or Invasion the public Safety may require it." Article First, § 12 of the Connecticut Constitution holds that "[t]he privileges of the writ of habeas corpus shall not be suspended, unless, when in case of rebellion or invasion, the public safety may require it; nor in any case, but by the legislature." The state constitutional right is implemented through General Statutes § 52-466, et seq. and Practice Book

§ 23-21, et seq.

"The principal purpose of the writ of habeas corpus is to serve as 'a bulwark against convictions that violate "fundamental fairness.""" Bunkley v. Commissioner, 222 Conn. 444, 460-61 (1992)(quoting Engle v. Isaac, 456 U.S. 107, 127 (1982)), overruled in part on other grounds, Small v. Commissioner, 286 Conn. 707, 723-24, cert. denied sub nom., Small v. Lantz, 555 U.S. 975 (2008). "In order to demonstrate such a fundamental unfairness or miscarriage of justice, the petitioner [must] show that he is burdened by an unreliable conviction." Bunkley v. Commissioner, 222 Conn. at 461.

a. Ineffective Assistance of Counsel at Trial

The Sixth Amendment to the United States Constitution and Article First, § 8 of the Connecticut Constitution guarantee the effective assistance of counsel. Gideon v. Wainwright, 372 U.S. 335 (1963); Strickland v. Washington, 466 U.S. 668 (1984); Siemon v. Stoughton, 184 Conn. 547, 554 (1981)(Article First, § 8 guarantees effective assistance of counsel); see also Woods v. Commissioner, 85 Conn. App. 544, 549 (same), cert. denied, 272 Conn. 903 (2004).

The test for ineffective assistance of counsel at trial is set forth in Strickland v. Washington, 466 U.S. 668 (1984). The test requires the petitioner to establish that counsel's performance was deficient and that the deficient performance prejudiced the defense. Strickland v. Washington, 466 U.S. at 687-94; see Phillips v. Warden, 220 Conn. 112, 132 (1991)(claim of ineffective assistance of counsel requires petitioner to establish deficient performance and actual prejudice); see also Gonzalez v. Commissioner, 308 Conn. 463, 470 (2013); Michael T. v. Commissioner, 307 Conn. 84, 91 (2012).

"'Unless a [habeas petitioner] [satisfies] both [Strickland prongs], it cannot be said that the conviction ... resulted from a breakdown in the adversary process that renders the result unreliable.'" Aillon v. Meachum, 211 Conn. 352, 357 (1989)(quoting Strickland, 466 U.S. at 687).

The habeas court can reject a claim of ineffective assistance of counsel on either prong of Strickland. See

Strickland, 466 U.S. at 697; Nardini v. Manson, 207 Conn. 118, 124 (1988).

i. Deficient Performance

Strickland's "performance prong" is well settled. Counsel's performance is deficient when counsel's "representation was not reasonably competent or within the range of competence displayed by lawyers with ordinary training and skill in the criminal law." (internal quotation marks omitted; citation omitted) Sastrom v. Mullaney, 286 Conn. 655, 662 (2008); see Strickland, 466 U.S. at 687-91; see also Gonzalez v. Commissioner, 308 Conn. at 470; Michael T. v. Commissioner, 307 Conn. at 91; State v. Clark, 170 Conn. 273, 283, cert. denied, 425 U.S. 962 (1976); Phillips v. Warden, 220 Conn. at 132 (performance deficient in the sense that counsel "'made errors so serious that counsel was not functioning as the "counsel" guaranteed by the Sixth Amendment'" (quoting Strickland, 466 U.S. at 687)). The petitioner "must show that counsel's representation fell below an objective standard of reasonableness." Strickland, 466 U.S. at 688; see Gonzalez, 308 Conn. at 484.

"The proper measure of attorney performance [is] simply reasonableness under prevailing professional norms." Strickland, 466 U.S. at 688. Hence, "in any case presenting an ineffectiveness claim, the performance inquiry must be whether counsel's assistance was reasonable considering all the circumstances. Prevailing norms of practice as reflected in American Bar Association standards and the like ... are guides to determining what is reasonable, but they are only guides. No particular set of detailed rules for counsel's conduct can satisfactorily take account of the variety of circumstances faced by defense counsel or the range of legitimate decisions regarding how best to represent a criminal defendant." Strickland, 466 U.S. at 688-89; see Phillips, 220 Conn. at 134; see also Missouri v. Frye, 566 U.S. ___, ___, 132 S.Ct. 1399, 1408 (2012)("codified standards of professional practice ... can be important guides").

The habeas court's "scrutiny of counsel's performance [is] highly deferential.... [The] court [will] judge the reasonableness of counsel's challenged conduct on the facts of the particular case, viewed as of the time of counsel's conduct. A convicted defendant making a claim of ineffective assistance [will have to] identify the acts or omissions of counsel that are alleged not to have been the result of reasonable professional judgment. The court [will] then determine whether, in light of all the circumstances, the identified acts or omissions were outside the range of professionally competent assistance."

Strickland, 466 U.S. at 689-90; see Gonzalez, 308 Conn. at 485.

In making this determination, "counsel is strongly presumed to have rendered adequate assistance and made all significant decisions in the exercise of reasonable professional judgment." Strickland, 466 U.S. at 690; see Sanders v. Commissioner, 83 Conn. App. 543, 551, cert. denied, 271 Conn. 914 (2004); see also Strickland, 466 U.S. at 689 ("a court must indulge a strong presumption that counsel's conduct falls within the wide range of reasonable professional assistance; that is, the defendant must overcome the presumption that, under the circumstances, the challenged action 'might be considered sound trial strategy'").

Finally, counsel's performance is measured without regard to whether counsel was court-appointed or privately retained. This is because "there is no sliding scale embedded in the constitution, affording financially capable defendants any more or less constitutional protection than indigent defendants who are served by appointed counsel." Skakel v. Warden, Tolland J.D., at Rockville, Docket No. CV-10-4003762 (Bishop, J.T.R), Mem. of Dec., Oct. 23, 2013, p. 13; see also Cuyler v. Sullivan, 446 U.S. 335, 344-45 (1980)("no basis for drawing a distinction between retained and appointed counsel"); Myers v.

Manson, 192 Conn. 383 (1984); cf. Strickland, 466 U.S. at 685 ("An accused is entitled to be assisted by an attorney, whether retained or appointed, who plays the role necessary to ensure that the trial is fair.").

ii. Prejudice

Prejudice results when "counsel's errors [are] so serious as to deprive the [petitioner] of a fair trial, a trial whose result is reliable." (internal quotation marks omitted) Strickland, 466 U.S. at 687; see Michael T., 307 Conn. at 101. Put differently, prejudice results when "there is a reasonable probability that, but for counsel's unprofessional errors, the result of the proceeding would have been different." Strickland, 466 U.S. at 694; see also Bunkley, 222 Conn. at 445; Phillips, 220 Conn. at 132. "[A] 'reasonable probability that, but for counsel's unprofessional errors, the result of the proceeding would have been different,' does not require the petitioner to show that 'counsel's deficient conduct more likely than not altered the outcome of the case.'" Bunkley, 222 Conn. at 445 (quoting Strickland, 466 U.S. at 693). "Rather, it merely requires the petitioner to establish 'a probability sufficient to undermine confidence in the outcome.'" Bunkley, 222 Conn. at 445-46 (quoting Strickland, 466 U.S. at 694); see also Gaines v. Commissioner, 306 Conn. 664, 688

(2012)("'[T]he question is whether there is a reasonable probability that, absent the [alleged] errors, the [fact finder] would have had a reasonable doubt respecting guilt.'" (quoting Strickland, 466 U.S. at 695)).

In determining prejudice, the habeas court must consider the totality of the original trial evidence, whether counsel's error has a "pervasive effect" on the evidence or just an "isolated, trivial effect," and whether the verdict enjoys "weak[]" record support or "overwhelming" record support. See Gaines v. Commissioner, 306 Conn. at 688-89 (citing Strickland, 466 U.S. at 695-96); see also Bryant v. Commissioner, 290 Conn. 502, 519 n.11 ("We recognize that the strength of the state's case bears most significantly to our analysis under the prejudice prong of Strickland."), cert. denied sub nom., Murphy v. Bryant, 558 U.S. 938 (2009).

In that "[t]he fundamental purpose of the constitutional requirement of effective assistance of counsel is 'to ensure that the trial is fair[,]'" Phillips, 220 Conn. at 134 (quoting Strickland, 466 U.S. at 685), "[t]he 'ultimate focus of the inquiry must be on the fundamental fairness of the proceeding whose result is being challenged.'" Id. (quoting Strickland, 466 U.S. at 696).

iii. Burden of Proof

The petitioner bears the burden of proof on any allegation of ineffective assistance of counsel, see Evans v. Warden, 29 Conn. App. 274, 278 (1992), and the standard of proof is a fair preponderance of the evidence. Gaines, 306 Conn. at 666.

iv. Cumulative Error

Non-constitutional errors cannot be aggregated to establish deficient performance or prejudice. See Anderson v. Commissioner, 148 Conn. App. 641, 644-46 (2014); see also Diaz v. Commissioner, 125 Conn. App. 57, 72 (2010), cert. denied, 299 Conn. 926 (2011); Adorno v. Commissioner, 66 Conn. App. 179, 195 n.7, cert. denied, 258 Conn. 943 (2001); but see Bourjaily v. United States, 483 U.S. 171, 179-80 (1987)("[I]ndividual pieces of evidence, insufficient in themselves to prove a point, may in cumulation prove it. The sum of an evidentiary presentation may well be greater than its constituent parts.").

Whether *constitutional* errors can be aggregated to find deficient performance and prejudice and thus ineffective assistance of counsel, has not been decided in Connecticut. However, federal authority supports the conclusion that such errors can be aggregated to satisfy Strickland. First, Strickland itself states that a petitioner "must show that there is a reasonable probability that but for counsel's unprofessional errors, the result of the proceeding would have been different." Strickland, 466 U.S. at 694. If each error had to be assessed separately to determine prejudice, there would be no reason for the Supreme Court to refer to errors in the plural. Second, in Murray v. Carrier, 477 U.S. 478 (1986), the Supreme Court stated that "the right to effective assistance of counsel ... may in a particular case be violated by even an isolated error of counsel if that error is sufficiently egregious and prejudicial." Id. at 497. If ineffective assistance of counsel can stem from an isolated error, then it follows that ineffective assistance of counsel can stem from multiple errors." Third, the Second Circuit held in Lindstadt v. Keane, 239 F.3d 191, 199 (2nd Cir. 2001): "We need not decide whether one or another or less than all of these four errors would suffice, because Strickland directs us to look at the 'totality of the evidence before the judge or jury,' keeping in mind that '[s]ome errors [] have ... a pervasive effect on the inferences to be drawn from the evidence, altering the evidentiary picture....' Id. at 695-96. We therefore consider these errors in the aggregate. See Moore v. Johnson, 194 F.3d 586, 619 (5th Cir. 1999)(holding that court should examine cumulative effect of errors committed by counsel across both the trial and sentencing)[.]" Citing Lindstadt, the Second Circuit concluded in Pavel v. Hollins, 261 F.3d 210, 216, 225-28 (2nd Cir. 2001), that the cumulative weight of trial counsel's constitutional missteps established deficient performance and that the defense was prejudiced. Thus, errors by counsel that are of constitutional dimension can and should be aggregated to establish deficient performance and prejudice under Strickland. A concise discussion of "cumulative error" can be found in J. Burkoff & N. Burkoff, Ineffective Assistance of Counsel (2012 Ed.), § 5:29, et seq.

v. Structural Error & Per Se Prejudice

In performing harmless error analysis of constitutional violations in direct appeal and habeas corpus cases, the United States Supreme Court has long held that "[s]ome constitutional violations ... by their very nature cast so much doubt on the fairness of the trial process that, as a matter of law, they can never be considered harmless." Satterwhite v. Texas, 486 U.S. 249, 256 (1988); accord Sullivan v Louisiana, 508 U.S. 275, 279 (1993) ("Although most constitutional errors have been held amenable to harmless error analysis, ... some will always invalidate the conviction."); Rose v. Clark, 478 U.S. 570, 577-78 (1986)("some constitutional errors require reversal without regard to the evidence in the particular case ...

[because they] render a trial fundamentally unfair"); Chapman v. California, 386 U.S. 18, 23 (1967)("there are some constitutional rights so basic to a fair trial that their infraction can never be treated as harmless error").

In Arizona v. Fulminante, 499 U.S. 279 (1991), the Court elucidated this rule of *per se* prejudice or *automatic reversal* by differentiating between the concepts of "structural" and "trial" error: "structural defects in the constitution of the trial mechanism," 499 U.S. at 309, are *per se* prejudicial; trial errors occurring "during the presentation of the case to the jury," Id. at 307, are subject to harmless error analysis. Id. at 307-08.

In Brecht v. Abrahamson, 507 U.S. 619 (1993), the Supreme Court changed the standard that applies in habeas cases for determining the harmlessness of constitutional "trial" errors. However, the Court did not change, and in fact reaffirmed, its longstanding doctrine treating "structural" errors as not subject to harmless error analysis and accordingly as prejudicial – hence reversible – per se:

> Trial error "occur[s] during the presentation of the case to the jury," and is amenable to harmless-error analysis because it "may ... be quantitatively assessed in the context of other evidence presented in order to

determine [the effect it had on the trial]." At the other end of the spectrum of constitutional errors lie "structural defects in the constitution of the trial mechanism, which defy analysis by 'harmless-error' standards." The existence of such defects – deprivation of the right to counsel, for example – requires automatic reversal of the conviction because they infect the entire trial process.

...

For the foregoing reasons, then, that the Kotteakos harmless-error standard applies in determining whether habeas relief must be granted because of constitutional error of the trial type."

Brecht v. Abrahamson, 507 U.S. at 629-30, 638 (quoting Fulminante, 499 U.S. at 307-08, and discussing Kotteakos v. United States, 328 U.S. 750 (1946)).

The denial of counsel at a critical stage of the proceedings, of course, constitutes structural error and per se prejudice. See Sullivan v. Louisiana, 508 U.S. at 279 ("total deprivation of the right to counsel"); see also Delaware v. Van Arsdall, 475 U.S. 673, 681 (1986)("[W]e have observed that some constitutional errors—such as denying a defendant the assistance of counsel at trial, or compelling him to stand trial before a trier of fact with a financial stake in the outcome—are so fundamental and pervasive that they require reversal without regard to the facts or circumstances of the particular case."). But ineffective assistance of counsel in some instances can also constitute structural error and per se prejudice. Decided the same day as Strickland, the Supreme Court held in United States v. Cronic, 466 U.S. 648 (1984), that prejudice is presumed when counsel "entirely fails to subject the prosecution's case to meaningful adversarial testing." 466 U.S. at 659. The failure, however, must be "complete." Bell v. Crone, 535 U.S. 685, 697 (2002). Counsel must be found to have provided virtually "no representation at all...." Moss v. Hofbauer, 286 F.3d 851, 861 (6th Cir.), cert. denied, 537 U.S. 1092 (2002).

Connecticut cases that discuss or find structural error and per se prejudice are State v. Ralph B., __ Conn. App. __, No. AC 35654 (Jan. 25, 2016); Davis v. Commissioner, Conn. __, No. SC 19286 (Nov. 17, 2015); State v. Brown, 279 Conn. 493, 509-10 (2006), and State v. Lopez, 271 Conn. 224, 226-38 (2004).

b. Ineffective Assistance of Counsel at Sentencing

"[A] criminal defendant has a constitutional right to effective assistance of counsel during the sentencing stage and a constitutional right not to be sentenced on the basis of improper factors or erroneous information." State v. Patterson, 236 Conn. 561, 573 (1996); see Mempa v. Rhay, 389 U.S. 128 (1967)(constitutional right to counsel at sentencing); Hilton v. Commissioner, 161 Conn. App. 58, 77 (2015).

Counsel's representation at sentencing "is an extremely important part of the complete defense...." ABA Standards for Criminal Justice, Defense Function (3rd Ed. 1993), Standard 4-8.1, Commentary. "[T]he Supreme Court has even suggested that the need for counsel may be greater at sentencing than in the determination of guilt because '[t]here a judge usually moves within a large area of discretion and doubts. ... Even the most self-assured judge may well want to bring to his aid every consideration that counsel for the accused can appropriately urge.'" Id. (quoting Carter v. Illinois, 329 U.S. 173, 178 (1946)). Thus, "effective defense counsel will present to the court all relevant mitigating material consistent with the defendant's best interests and will ensure that all information presented to the court by the state meets the standards of reliability and relevance applicable during sentencing." State v. Patterson, 236 Conn. at 573.

Standard 4-8.1(b) of the ABA Standards for Criminal Justice, Defense Function (3rd Ed. 1993) provides in pertinent part:

> *Defense counsel should present to the court any ground which will assist in reaching a proper disposition favorable to the accused. If a presentence report or summary is made available to defense counsel, he or she should seek to verify the information contained in it and should be prepared to supplement or challenge it if necessary. If there is no presentence report or if it is not disclosed, defense counsel should submit to the court and the prosecutor all favorable information relevant to sentencing....*

A claim of ineffective assistance of counsel at sentencing is analyzed under the two-pronged Strickland test. First, the petitioner must demonstrate that counsel's performance was deficient, in that it "fell below an objective standard of reasonableness." Strickland, 466 U.S. at 688; see Davis v. Commissioner, __ Conn. __, __, No. SC 19286 (Nov. 17, 2015). Second, the petitioner must demonstrate that "actual prejudice" resulted. This requires the petitioner to establish "a reasonable probability that, but for counsel's unprofessional errors, the result of the proceeding would have been different." Strickland, 466 U.S. at 694; see Davis v. Commissioner, __ Conn. at __, No.

SC 19286 (Nov. 17, 2015); see also Vega v. Commissioner, 103 Conn. App. 732, 734 (2007)("[I]t is not enough for the [petitioner] to show that the errors [made by counsel] had some conceivable effect on the outcome of the proceeding.... Rather, [the petitioner] must show that there is a reasonable probability that, but for counsel's unprofessional errors, the result of the proceeding would have been different." (internal quotation marks omitted; citation omitted)), cert. denied, 285 Conn. 905 (2008). However, if counsel's deficient performance at sentencing "fails to subject the prosecution's case to meaningful adversarial testing" or otherwise constitutes an "actual breakdown in the adversarial process," prejudice is presumed under United States v. Cronic, 466 U.S. 648, 655-60 (1984). See Davis, __ Conn. at __, No. SC 19286 (Nov. 17, 2015)(prejudice presumed under Cronic where defense counsel at sentencing agreed with the State's recommendation that the maximum sentence under the plea agreement be imposed). Per se prejudice at sentencing and Cronic's application is discussed in Bell v. Cone, 535 U.S. 685, 697 (2002).

The following recent Connecticut cases concern a claim of ineffective assistance of counsel at sentencing: Davis v. Commissioner, supra, __ Conn. __, No. SC 19286 (Nov. 17, 2015)(ineffectiveness found for complete failure to advocate for lesser sentence); <u>Hilton v. Commissioner</u>, 161 Conn. App. at 76-78 (ineffectiveness not found for failure to present relatives who would have commented on petitioner's positive attributes); <u>Vega v. Commissioner</u>, 103 Conn. App. 732, 734 (2007)(ineffectiveness not found for failure to present mitigating evidence, specifically, psychiatric evaluation), <u>cert. denied</u>, 285 Conn. 905 (2008).

For further discussion on deficiencies of counsel related to sentencing, see <u>infra</u> R. *AMENDED PETITION* 3.a.ii. *For Sentencing*.

A defendant also has a constitutional right to effective assistance of counsel at the sentence review hearing authorized under General Statutes § 51-195 and Practice Book § 43-23, et seq. <u>See</u> <u>Consiglio v. Warden</u>, 153 Conn. 673 (1966)(right to effective assistance of counsel at sentence review). An adjunct to the right to effective assistance of counsel at sentence review is the right to be informed of the right to sentence review and, if such review is desired, to have the application timely filed and perfected. <u>See</u> General Statutes § 51-195; Practice Book § 43-23, et seq. <u>Strickland</u>'s two-pronged inquiry applies to ineffective assistance of counsel claims that concern sentence review. <u>See</u> <u>Hilton</u>, 161 Conn. App. at 81 (claim of failure to file petitioner's sentence review application analyzed under <u>Strickland</u>). If the evidence indicates that the petitioner was aware of the right to sentence review, the petitioner must demonstrate that he desired sentence review and that he communicated his desire to counsel. See Id.; see also James L. v. Commissioner, 245 Conn. 132, 136-48 (1998); Eastwood v. Commissioner, 114 Conn. App. 471, 484, cert. denied, 292 Conn. 918 (2009); Andres v. Commissioner of Correction, 108 Conn. App. 509, 513-16, cert. denied, 289 Conn. 906 (2008); Valentin v. Commissioner, 94 Conn. App. 751, 758 (2006); Ramos v. Commissioner, 67 Conn. App. 654, 667, cert. denied, 260 Conn. 912 (2002). The habeas court has the authority to restore the petitioner's right to sentence review where it has been shown that the petitioner wanted sentence review and that counsel's breach prevented him or her from receiving it. See James L. Commissioner, 245 Conn. at 136-48; see also Janulawicz v. Commissioner, 310 Conn. 265 (2013).

c. Ineffective Assistance of Counsel on Appeal

A defendant who has suffered a judgment of conviction has a statutory right to appeal, see General Statutes §§ 51-197a to 51-197f, 54-94a, 54-95, see also Practice Book § 60-1, et seq.; see also Ghant v. Commissioner, 255 Conn. 1, 17-18 (2000)(claim that Connecticut Constitution guarantees right to appeal not briefed or argued), overruled in part on other grounds, State v. Elson, 311 Conn. 726 (2014), and, if indigent, the constitutional right to counsel in the first appeal as of right. Douglas v. California, 372 U.S. 353 (1963); see also General Statutes § 52-296b; Practice Book §§ 62-8, 63-1, 63-5 and 6307. An adjunct to the constitutional right to counsel on the initial appeal is the constitutional right to effective assistance of counsel on the appeal. Evitts v. Lucey, 469 U.S. 387 (1985)(right to effective assistance of counsel applies on an appeal as of right); accord Small v. Commissioner, 286 Conn. 707, 712 (2008). The Strickland standard applies to claims of ineffective assistance of appellate counsel. Smith v. Murray, 477 U.S. 527, 535-36 (1986)(applying Strickland to claim of attorney error on appeal); see also Sekou v. Warden, 216 Conn. 678, 690 (1990).

On the performance prong, the petitioner must "show that [appellate] counsel was objectively unreasonable, see Strickland, 466 U.S., at 687-691, in failing to find arguable issues to appeal—that is, that counsel unreasonably failed to discover nonfrivolous issues and to file a merits brief raising them." Smith v. Robbins, 528 U.S. 259, 285 (2000); cf. Murray v. Carrier, 477 U.S. 478, 492 (1986)(hearing will inquire "into counsel's state of mind in failing to raise a claim on appeal"). "If the issues not raised by ... appellate counsel lack merit, [the petitioner] cannot [satisfy the performance prong] since the failure to pursue unmeritorious claims cannot be considered conduct falling below the level of reasonably competent representation." Sekou v. Warden, 216 Conn. at 690.

On the prejudice prong, the petitioner "must show a reasonable probability that, but for his counsel's [error], he would have prevailed on his appeal." Smith v. Robbins, 528 U.S. at 285 (citing Strickland, 466 U.S. at 694); accord Small, 286 Conn. at 717-24, 728; see, e.g. Small, 286 Conn. at 731 ("petitioner's claim of ineffective assistance of appellate counsel must fail because he could not demonstrate a reasonable probability that, on appeal, the state could not have met its burden of showing that the omitted instruction was harmless beyond a reasonable doubt").

An adjunct to the right to effective assistance of counsel on appeal is the right to be informed of the right to appeal. Thus, trial counsel or appellate counsel has "a constitutional obligation to advise [the] defendant of appeal rights when either (1) the defendant has reasonably demonstrated to counsel his or her interest in filing an appeal, or (2) a rational defendant would want to appeal under the circumstances." Ghant v. Commissioner, 255 Conn. at 7 (citing Roe v. Flores-Ortega, 528 U.S. 470, 480 (2000)), overruled in part on other grounds, State v. Elson, supra, 311 Conn. 726; see also ABA Standards for Criminal

Justice, Defense Function (3rd Ed. 1993), Standard 4-8.2 *Appeal* ("(a) After conviction, defense counsel should explain to the defendant the meaning and consequences of the court's judgment and defendant's right of appeal."). The failure to do so may constitute deficient performance under Strickland. See Ghant, 255 Conn. at 8-10. Prejudice under Strickland is demonstrated when "'there is a reasonable probability that, but for counsel's deficient failure to consult with [the defendant] about an appeal, [the defendant] would have timely appealed.'" Ghant, 255 Conn. at 10 (quoting Roe v. Flores-Ortega, 528 U.S. at 484). The remedy when both prongs of Strickland are met is the habeas court's restoration of the petitioner's appellate rights. See Ghant, 255 Conn. at 2-18 (recognizing the authority of the habeas court to restore appellate rights, but finding that the two-part Roe test was not met and that the restoration was clearly erroneous); cf. State v. Phidd, 42 Conn. App. 17, 27-29 (habeas court empowered restore petitioner's appellate rights where petitioner knew of the right, but no appeal was taken due to counsel's ineffectiveness), cert. denied, 238 Conn. 907 (1996), cert. denied, 520 U.S. 1108 (1997). However, before a petitioner can pursue a restoration of his or her appellate rights from the habeas court, the petitioner must file in the Connecticut Appellate Court or Connecticut Supreme

Court, as the case may be, a motion for permission to file a late appeal under Practice Book §§ 60-2 and 60-3 and must fail on the motion. See Janulawicz v. Commissioner, 310 Conn. 265 (2013); Ramos v. Commissioner, 248 Conn. 52 (1999).

The failure of trial counsel or appellate counsel to advise the defendant of the consequences of waiving an appeal may constitute ineffective assistance of counsel. Such failure may also render the defendant's waiver involuntary and unintelligent and, hence, invalid. See Barlow v. Lopes, 201 Conn. 103 (1986). Likewise, the failure of appellate counsel to advise the defendant of the consequences of withdrawing an appeal may constitute ineffective assistance of counsel and/or render the decision to withdraw involuntary and unintelligent and, thus, invalid. For a discussion of a petitioner's ability to obtain through a habeas petition reinstatement of a withdrawn appeal, see Kaddah v. Commissioner, 299 Conn. 129 (2010).

d. Ineffective Assistance of Counsel on Guilty Plea

i. Generally

A defendant has a constitutional right to effective

assistance of counsel on a guilty plea. Hill v. Lockhart, 474 U.S. 52, 57 (1985); see Copas v. Commissioner, 234 Conn. 139, 153 (1995), overruled in part on other grounds, Washington v. Commissioner, 287 Conn. 792 (2008); Ebron v. Commissioner, 120 Conn. App. 560, 566-67 (2010), rev'd in part on other grounds, 307 Conn. 342 (2012), cert. denied in part on other grounds sub. nom., Arnone v. Ebron, __ U.S. __, 133 S.Ct. 1726 (2013). If a guilty plea rests on defense counsel's advice and that advice was erroneous or not "within the range of competence demanded of attorneys in criminal cases[,]" McMann v. Richardson, 397 U.S. 759, 771 (1970), the plea may be involuntary, see North Carolina v. Alford, 400 U.S. 25, 31 (1970)("plea [must] represent[] a voluntary and intelligent choice among the alternative courses of action"), and, hence, invalid because it is the product of ineffective assistance of counsel. Hill v. Lockhart, 474 U.S. at 56-57.

In Hill v. Lockhart, supra, 474 U.S. 52, the Supreme Court held that claims of ineffective assistance of counsel on a guilty plea must be evaluated under the Strickland standard. 474 U.S. at 57-59. However, because the claim concerns a plea and not defense counsel's performance at trial, the Supreme Court modified the prejudice prong by requiring the petitioner to show "that there is a reasonable probability that, but for counsel's errors, he would not have pleaded guilty and would have insisted on going to trial." 474 U.S. at 59; see Carraway v. Commissioner, 317 Conn. 594, 599-600 (2015)(on Strickland's prejudice prong the petitioner must show that but for counsel's deficient performance he would have insisted on proceeding to trial); Washington v. Commissioner, 287 Conn. at 835 ("In the context of a guilty plea ... to succeed on the prejudice prong the petitioner must demonstrate that, but for counsel's alleged ineffective performance, the petitioner would not have pleaded guilty and would have proceeded to trial."); see also Crawford v. Commissioner, 285 Conn. 585, 598 (2008); Johnson v. Commissioner, 285 Conn. 556, 576 (2008); D'Amico v. Manson, 193 Conn. 144, 153-57 (1984)(petitioner must allege and prove that but for the misunderstanding, he would not have pleaded guilty).

In deciding whether the petitioner would have gone to trial absent defense counsel's deficient performance, the habeas court must consider, among other things, whether counsel's advice or recommendation would have been different if counsel had taken the appropriate steps. See Hill, 474 U.S. at 58-59 ("the determination whether the error 'prejudiced' the defendant ... will depend on the likelihood that discovery of the evidence would have led counsel to change his recommendation as to the plea"); see also Carraway v. Commissioner, 144 Conn. App. 461,

471-77 (2013), appeal dismissed, 317 Conn. 594 (2015). Whether the trial would have resulted in an outcome more favorable than that produced by the guilty plea is a relevant consideration only insofar as it bears on what defense counsel's advice would have been or might have been had counsel taken the appropriate steps. See Carraway v. Commissioner, 144 Conn. App. at 474 ("The prospect of an acquittal, or a more favorable sentence after trial, is clearly relevant in considering whether counsel's advice with respect to a plea offer would have changed had he not performed deficiently; indeed, it may be the single most important consideration.")

Copas v. Commissioner, supra, 234 Conn. 139, which held that "the petitioner [must] demonstrate that he would not have pleaded guilty, that he would have insisted on going to trial, *and that the evidence that had been undiscovered or the defenses he claims should have been introduced were likely to have been successful at trial*[,]" (emphasis added) 234 Conn. at 151, was overruled sub silencio in subsequent Connecticut Supreme court cases. See Washington v. Commissioner, 287 Conn. at 835; Crawford v. Commissioner, 285 Conn. at 598. Thus, the likelihood of success at trial is no longer an element that the habeas petitioner must prove. It is only a consideration insofar as it bears on what counsel's advice would have been had he or she performed differently. See Carraway, 317 Conn. at 599-600 and n.6; see also Carraway, 144 Conn. App. at 471-77.

A recommendation by defense counsel to plead guilty that is not preceded by an adequate investigation of the facts and an exploration of the possible defenses constitutes deficient performance under Strickland. See, e.g. Copas, supra, 234 Conn. 139 (counsel deficient because he failed to investigate defendant's mental illness and to assess viability of mental state defense); cf. Von Moltke v. Gillies, 332 U.S. 708, 721 (1948)("Prior to trial an accused is entitled to rely upon his counsel to make an independent examination of the facts, circumstances, pleadings and laws involved and then to offer his informed opinion as to what plea should be entered.").

ii. Direct Consequences

"The longstanding test for determining the validity of a guilty plea is 'whether the plea represents a voluntary and intelligent choice among the alternative courses of action open to the defendant.'" Hill v. Lockhart, 474 U.S. at 56 (quoting North Carolina v. Alford, 400 U.S. at 31); see also Practice Book Section 39-20 (court must determine that guilty plea is voluntary before accepting it). Accordingly, before a guilty plea is entered, the defendant must be aware of the direct consequences of the plea. Brady v. United States, 397 U.S. 742, 748 (1970); see Falby v. Commissioner, 32 Conn. App. 438, 445 ("A defendant must be aware of all direct consequences of his plea."), cert. denied, 227 Conn. 927 (1993). A direct consequence of a guilty plea is the punishment to be exacted. See State v. Lloyd, 8 Conn. App. 491, 494 (1986), cert. denied and cross-pet. denied, 203 Conn. 801 (1987).

Practice Book § 39-19 identifies the direct consequences of a guilty plea, see Falby v. Commissioner, 32 Conn. App. at 445, and sets forth the scope of the Court's canvass. Before the plea is accepted, the Court must determine that the defendant understands "[t]he nature of the charge;" § 39-19(1), "[t]he mandatory minimum sentence, if any;" § 39-19(2), "[t]he fact that the statute for the ... offense does not permit the sentence to be suspended;" § 39-19(3), "[t]he maximum possible sentence on the charge, including, if there are several charges, the maximum sentence possible from consecutive sentences and, including, when applicable, the fact that a different or additional punishment may be authorized by reason of a previous conviction;" § 39-19(4), and "[t]he fact that he or she has the right to plead not guilty or to persist in that plea if it has already been made, and the fact that he or she has the right to be tried by a jury or a judge and that at that trial the defendant has the right to the assistance of counsel, the right to confront and cross-examine witnesses against him or her, and the right not to be compelled to incriminate himself or herself." § 39-19(5); see also Boykin v. Alabama, 395 U.S. 238, 244 (1969)(court "must make sure [the defendant] has a full understanding of what the plea connotes and its consequences").

Defense counsel is likewise obligated to discuss with the defendant the direct consequences of an anticipated guilty plea. Without such discussion the defendant cannot make a fully informed decision concerning the alternatives he or she faces. Consequently, the failure to discuss the plea's direct consequences may constitute ineffective assistance of counsel.

A habeas petition that alleges ineffective assistance of counsel on a guilty plea due to erroneous advice on a direct consequence of the plea should also allege, in a separate count, that the plea is involuntary and, hence, invalid. This is the prudent approach notwithstanding case law indicating that "in certain circumstances, a petitioner's claim of a constitutional violation is so inextricably bound up in the issue of the effectiveness of trial counsel, that a separate claim of a constitutional violation is not required."

Carpenter v. Commissioner, 274 Conn. 834, 843 (2005).

iii. Immigration Consequences

Defense counsel's failure to advise the defendant of the collateral consequences of a change of plea, specifically, the immigration consequences, may constitute deficient performance under Strickland. In Padilla v. Kentucky, 559 U.S. 356, 364-69 (2010), the Supreme Court set aside a guilty plea, holding that counsel's failure to correctly inform the defendant of the immigration consequences of the plea amounted to constitutionally deficient assistance. The plea, however, will not be set aside unless prejudice under Strickland is also shown.

Following Padilla v. Kentucky, supra, 559 U.S. 356, the Supreme Court held that Padilla does not have retroactive application to any conviction that became final before Padilla was decided. This is because Padilla declared a new rule. See Chaidez v. United States, 568 U.S. __, __, 133 S.Ct. 1103, 1106-13 (2013). Subsequently, the Connecticut Supreme Court held that Padilla does not apply retroactively as a matter of Connecticut law. Theirsaint v. Commissioner, 316 Conn. 89, 106-24 (2015); see also Alcena v. Commissioner, 146 Conn. App. 370, 374 ("Padilla is not subject to retroactive application"), cert. denied, 310 Conn. 948 (2013).

In assessing a <u>Padilla</u> claim, habeas counsel should also consult General Statutes § 54-1j. Subsection (c) of General Statutes § 54-1j may offer an alternative form of relief, namely, a motion to vacate the plea, which would be filed in the trial court.

iv. Indirect or Collateral Consequences

"There is no requirement ... that the defendant be advised of every possible consequence of ... a plea." <u>State v. Gilnite</u>, 202 Conn. 369, 383 (1987). Thus, a guilty plea motivated by defense counsel's erroneous advice on an indirect or collateral consequence does not render the plea involuntary and unintelligent and, hence, invalid. The erroneous advice in such circumstances does not amount to ineffective assistance of counsel.

However, when the guilty plea is motivated by "gross misadvice" on an indirect or collateral consequence, ineffective assistance of counsel may be found and the plea may be invalidated. See <u>Hernandez v. Commissioner</u>, 82 Conn. App. 701, 709 (2010)("Where 'the petitioner relied on gross misadvice about an indirect consequence, his plea would have been involuntary, unintelligent and, therefore, invalid.'" (quoting <u>Falby</u>, 32 Conn. App. at 446-47)).

Parole eligibility is an indirect consequence. See <u>Hill v.</u>

Lockhart, 474 U.S. at 56 (federal constitution does not require States to supply a defendant with parole eligibility information in order for guilty plea to be voluntary). Erroneous advice on parole eligibility generally does not constitute ineffective assistance of counsel and, thus, does not vitiate the guilty plea. Hill, 474 U.S. 52 (1985). When, however, the erroneous advice amounts to "gross misadvice" ineffective assistance may be found and the plea invalidated. See, e.g. Hernandez v. Commissioner, supra, 82 Conn. App. 701 (advice that defendant would be parole eligible after serving 50 percent of murder sentence, when in fact defendant was completely ineligible for parole, constituted gross misadvice that amounted to ineffective assistance of counsel and rendered the plea involuntary and invalid).

Similarly, "parole board procedure is an indirect consequence of a guilty plea." Falby, 32 Conn. App. at 446. Erroneous advice concerning the nature of a parole board hearing is "ordinary error" and will not call the plea into question. The error must amount to "gross misadvice" before the plea will potentially be invalidated. See Id. at 442-48.

B. Custody

A necessary element of a habeas petition is that, at the time the petition is filed, the petitioner is in custody pursuant to the judgment under attack. See General Statutes § 52-466. Custody, once established, is not eviscerated by the expiration of the petitioner's incarceration, parole or probation. See Barlow v. Lopes, 201 Conn. 103, 105 n.2 (1986)(custody "'survives [the petitioner's] release from incarceration and parole'" (quoting Herbert v. Manson, 199 Conn. 143, 143-44 n.1 (1986))); see also Smith v. Commissioner, 65 Conn. App. 172, 176 (2001)("It is clear that a petition for writ of habeas corpus, if filed while the petitioner is in custody, is not rendered moot by the expiration of the petitioner's sentence."); Haynes v. Bronson, 13 Conn. App. 708, 710 (1988)("The petitioner was in custody at the time he filed his petition for habeas corpus. The expiration of his sentence prior to the decision of the [habeas court] did not render his claims moot."). Absent custody, the petition is subject to dismissal for lack of subject matter jurisdiction. Custody, thus, must be alleged in the petition.

Custody for habeas corpus purposes is also discussed in Ajadi v. Commissioner, 280 Conn. 514, 539 n.26 (2006); Oliphant v. Commissioner, 274 Conn. 563 (2005) ; Lebron v. Commissioner, 82 Conn. App. 475 (2004), aff'd, 274 Conn. 507 (2005), and Ford v. Commissioner, 59 Conn. App.

823 (2000).

If the petitioner is an alien who is subject to a final deportation order, the petitioner is in custody for habeas corpus purposes if he or she has not yet been deported under the order. See Simmonds v. I.N.S., 326 F.3d 351, 356 (2nd Cir. 2003); Aguilera v. Kirkpatrick, 241 F.3d 1286, 1291 (10th Cir. 2001); Mustata v. U.S. Dept. of Justice, 179 F.3d 1017, 1021 n.4 1999 FED App. 0221P (6th Cir. 1999). However, if he or she has been deported pursuant to the order, custody for habeas corpus purposes is not established. See Merlan v. Holder, 667 F.3d 538 (5th Cir. 2011); Kumarasamy v. Attorney General of U.S., 453 F.3d 169, 173 (3d Cir. 2006), as amended (Aug. 4, 2006); Patel v. U.S. Atty. Gen., 334 F.3d 1259, 1263 (11th Cir. 2003); Miranda v. Reno, 238 F.3d 1156, 1159 (9th Cir. 2001). See infra T. RESPONDENT'S DEFENSES 3. Mootness.

In Wilson v. Flaherty, 689 F.3d 332, 333 (4th Cir. 2012), the Fourth Circuit held that sex offender registration does not constitute custody for federal habeas corpus purposes. Whether such registration constitutes custody for state habeas corpus purposes has not been litigated in the Connecticut Appellate Court or Connecticut Supreme Court.

C. Venue

The venue for a habeas petition is determined according to General Statutes § 52-466. Subsection (a)(1) provides that "[a]n application for a writ of habeas corpus, other than an application pursuant to subdivision (2) of this subsection, shall be made to the superior court, or to a judge thereof, for the judicial district in which the person whose custody is in question is claimed to be illegally confined or deprived of such person's liberty." Subsection (a)(2) states that "[a]n application for a writ of habeas corpus claiming illegal confinement or deprivation of liberty, made by or on behalf of an inmate or prisoner confined in a correctional facility as a result of a conviction of a crime, shall be made to the superior court, or to a judge thereof, for the judicial district of Tolland." The statute is effectuated by Practice Book §§ 23-27 and 23-28.

When venue is the Judicial District of Tolland, the petition and all subsequent pleadings should be filed at the Superior Court, 20 Park Street, Rockville, CT 06066.

D. Statute of Limitations

The statute of limitations for a habeas petition is contained in General Statutes § 52-470(c)(d)(e)(f). Counsel must consult the statute when identifying, developing and drafting the habeas claims. Counsel is also urged to familiarize himself or herself with the one-year time limitation that governs federal habeas corpus petitions. See 28 U.S.C. § 2244(d)(1)(one-year statute of limitation).

CHAPTER 2.
PRO SE HABEAS PETITIONS

Habeas counsel should immediately obtain a copy of the pro se habeas petition. The pro se petition, along with the appellate opinion, often serves as habeas counsel's initial foray into the case. A pro se petition should never be rejected out of hand. Rather, the petition should be investigated and researched, as the claims may have merit. The merit or non-merit of the claims in the pro se petition should always be discussed with the client.

At the same time, habeas counsel should not limit his or her review to the claims in the pro se petition. A pro se petitioner generally lacks the legal knowledge to identify all the grounds for a collateral attack on the judgment. Habeas counsel, thus, should comb the entire record for meritorious claims.

CHAPTER 3.

COURT-APPOINTED HABEAS COUNSEL

Although an indigent petitioner has no federal constitutional right to counsel in a state collateral proceeding after exhaustion of direct appellate review, see Pennsylvania v. Finley, 481 U.S. 551 (1987); but see Coleman v. Thompson, 501 U.S. 722, 755-56 (1991)(may have federal constitutional right to counsel in initial state collateral proceeding if it is the first place ineffective assistance of counsel can be alleged); Martinez v. Ryan, 566 U.S. 1, __, 132 S.Ct. 1309, 1315-21 (2012)(same), he or she has a statutory right to counsel "in any habeas corpus proceeding arising from a criminal matter...." General Statutes § 51-296(a). Practice Book § 23-26 implements the statutory right.

The filing of a pro se habeas petition generally leads to the appointment of counsel under the statute, as most pro se petitioners are indigent. See Zollo v. Commissioner, 133 Conn. App. 266, 285 ("Generally, a petition for writ of habeas corpus is filed by a self-represented petitioner for whom a public defender is later appointed."), cert. granted on other grounds, 304 Conn. 910 (2012). Court-appointed habeas counsel must provide constitutionally effective representation. Lozada v. Warden, 223 Conn. 834 (1992). Court-appointed habeas counsel must also adhere to the Rules of Professional Conduct, in particular, Rule 1.1 *Competence*, Rule 1.3 *Diligence*, and Rule 1.4 *Communication*.

CHAPTER 4.

PRIVATELY RETAINED HABEAS COUNSEL

Privately retained habeas counsel, like court-appointed habeas counsel, must provide constitutionally effective representation. Habeas counsel must also adhere to the Rules of Professional Conduct, Rules 1.1, 1.3 and 1.4 in particular.

In any habeas case where counsel is retained, the legal fee and scope of the representation must be in writing unless the petitioner is a regular or long-standing client. See Rules of Professional Conduct, Rules 1.5 *Fees*; see also ABA Standards for Criminal Justice, Defense Function (3rd Ed. 1993), Standard 4-3.3 *Fees.* Putting the agreement in writing helps to create trust between the lawyer and client, especially the new client. Failing to put the agreement in writing serves neither party's interest and will only exacerbate the matter when the client claims faulty representation.

CHAPTER 5.
KEEPING THE CLIENT INFORMED

Keeping the client informed is essential to a healthy attorney-client relationship and to the success of the habeas case. The ABA Standards for Criminal Justice, Defense Function (3rd Ed. 1993) require that habeas counsel keep the petitioner informed about the status of the case. See Standard 4-3.8 *Duty to Keep Client Informed* ("keep the client informed"); Standard 4-5.1 *Advising the Accused* ("advise the accused with complete candor"). Rule 1.4 *Communication* of the Rules of Professional Conduct also requires that the client be kept informed about the status of the case and consulted when necessary. Rule 1.4(a)(1)(2)(3). The rule further requires counsel to provide an explanation of any issue that is necessary to an informed decision by the client. Rule 1.4(b).

CHAPTER 6.

AUTHORIZATIONS

Habeas counsel, whether retained or court-appointed, should secure from the client a signed authorization to obtain copies of the files of the attorneys who previously represented the client in the matter. This should be done without delay. Absent a signed authorization, the attorney has no legal obligation to turn over the file, or portions of it, to habeas counsel. The attorney can invoke the Rules of Professional Conduct, specifically, Rule 1.6(a)("lawyer shall not reveal information relating to representation of a client unless the client gives informed consent"), and Rule 1.9(c)("lawyer who has formerly represented a client in a matter ... shall not ... reveal information relating to the representation except as these Rules would permit or require").

In this regard, it is important to note the rule of

confidentiality enunciated in Rule 1.6 *Confidentiality of Information* and Rule 1.9 *Duties to Former Clients* of the Rules of Professional Conduct is broader than the attorney-client privilege which operates principally in the courtroom. The confidentiality rule "applies in situations other than those where evidence is sought from the lawyer through compulsion of law. The confidentiality [r]ule ... applies not only to matters communicated in confidence by the client but also to all information relating to the representation, whatever its source." Rule 1.6, Official Commentary. Accordingly, no copy of the client's file can be obtained from prior counsel unless an authorization satisfying Rule 1.6(a)'s informed consent provision is provided to prior counsel.

Once received, the signed authorization should be sent to prior counsel without delay. Disputes as to copy costs and shipping should be privately and equitably resolved. The Office of Chief Public Defender (OCPD) has occasionally offered to pay the copy costs in a court-appointed case where the file is voluminous and the cost of reproducing it would be too burdensome to prior counsel or to habeas counsel. If this circumstance arises, OCPD should be contacted before any in-house or out-sourced copying occurs.

CHAPTER 7.
OBTAINING FILES

A. Trial Counsel's File

a. Documents

Because "[t]he trial transcript seldom discloses all of the considerations of strategy that may have induced counsel to follow a particular course of action[,]" State v. Leecan, 198 Conn. 517, 541, cert. denied, 476 U.S. 1184 (1986), every effort should be made to obtain a copy of trial counsel's entire file. This should be done without delay by sending a letter to trial counsel, with an authorization signed by the client attached, demanding that a copy of the entire file be forwarded within 30 days to habeas counsel for purposes of the pending litigation. If the file is not timely received, habeas counsel should follow-up on the request by sending an additional letter to trial counsel and by calling trial counsel.

While it is a violation of the Rules of Professional Conduct to refuse a properly authorized request and to withhold a file, <u>see</u> Rule 1.16(d)("lawyer shall ... surrender[] papers and property to which the client is entitled), trial counsel need not disclose his or her entire file. Statewide Grievance Committee Ethics Opinion 84-3 identifies the portions of the file that must be turned over and those portions which can be withheld. Ethics Opinion 84-3, which is an adoption of Opinion 1977-3 of the San Diego Bar Association, reads in pertinent part as follows:

> *A typical client's file contains, broadly speaking, the following categories of documents:*
>
> *(a) pleadings and other papers filed with the court, which become part of the public record;*
>
> *(b) letters to the client, to the opposition, to witnesses, and to the attorney from the same;*
>
> *(c) notes written by the attorney to himself preparatory to drafting other documents or as preparation for disposition or notes of interviews—all typically characterized by their informality, candor, and containing mental impressions, conclusions, opinions, or legal theories;*
>
> *(d) investigative and research reports (legal and*

factual) prepared at the attorney's direction for the attorney's preparation of a particular matter.

Ethics Opinion 84-3.

The opinion holds that class (a) and class (b) documents must be turned over. As to class (d) documents, the opinion states that "[v]ariations among [the] documents are so numerous that it is not possible to comment generally about specifics. On the whole, however, investigative reports and written expert opinions should be turned over to the client." Ethics Opinion 84-3. As to class (c) documents—personal notes written by the attorney, the opinion holds that they are not the property of the client and that the client has no right to them. "This is so because the typical attorney-client relationship presupposes that the rough, blemished opinions of the attorney, whether or not reduced to writing, are the tools of his trade (likened to the tools of a carpenter) without which the attorney cannot construct the appropriate legal representation for which the client has retained him and which the client has every right to expect." Ethics Opinion 84-3.

Consequently, the relevant Rules Of Professional Conduct and Statewide Grievance Committee Ethics Opinion 84-3 should be consulted if trial counsel refuses to provide a copy of his or her entire file or otherwise seeks to withhold certain sections of it, as this may or may not be a proper stance for counsel to take. An objection, however, based on the attorney-client privilege (which is a common law evidentiary rule) or the work-product doctrine (which is a rule of discovery) is not valid because the objection lies with the client, not trial counsel. See Practice Book § 13-3 (civil work-product doctrine) and § 40-31 (criminal work-product doctrine); see also Spivey v. Zant, 683 F.2d 881, 885 (5th Cir. 1982)("the work product doctrine does not apply to the situation in which a client seeks access to documents or other tangible things created or amassed by his attorney during the course of the representation"); see also Code Of Evidence, Article V. Privileges and Author Commentary (j) Attorney/Client; see generally C. Tait & Hon. E. Prescott, Tait's Handbook Of Connecticut Evidence, § 5.20, et seq. (5th Ed. 2014)(Attorney-Client Privilege).

Notwithstanding Ethics Opinion 84-3's holding that counsel can withhold his or her notes, every effort should be made to convince trial counsel that it is in the best interest of the client (and counsel) to disclose the entire file, including counsel's notes, to habeas counsel. Simply put, the entire file will aid in determining "the reasonableness of counsel's challenged conduct on the facts of the particular case, viewed as of the time of counsel's conduct." <u>Strickland</u>, 466 U.S. at 689-90; <u>see</u> <u>Gonzalez</u>, 308 Conn. at 485; <u>see also</u> <u>Id.</u>, at 691 ("inquiry into counsel's conversations with the defendant may be critical to a proper assessment of counsel's investigation decisions, just as it may be critical to a proper assessment of counsel's other litigation decisions"); <u>cf.</u> <u>Maxwell v. Florida</u>, 479 U.S. 972 (1986)(Marshall, J., dissenting from denial of cert.)("There is no more accurate or reliable evidence of trial counsel's actual perspective and extent of preparation than the contents of his client's case file. Access to these materials is critical where ... trial counsel's testimony rests on little more than vague recollections.").

Finally, if trial counsel takes the position that Practice Book § 40-10(a) prohibits trial counsel from providing habeas counsel with a copy of the discovery received from the State, habeas counsel should move either the trial court or habeas court, pursuant to Practice Book § 40-10(a), for permission to receive the materials for the purpose of the habeas litigation.

b. Conversations

Trial counsel is not a party to the habeas, but rather an anticipated witness in the proceedings. Thus, counsel's rights and obligations differ from that of an attorney representing a client in a criminal trial or appeal. Trial counsel—even as a witness—has the right to be represented by an attorney. And to the extent such representation is secured, neither habeas counsel nor the State should directly contact or communicate with counsel. See Rules of Professional Conduct, Rule 4.2 *Communication with Person Represented by Counsel.*

Conversations between trial counsel and habeas counsel are permissible under Rule 1.6(d) of the Rules of Professional Conduct even without an authorization executed by the client. This is because Rule 1.6(d) provides that the "lawyer may reveal ... information [relating to representation of a client] ... to respond to allegations in any proceeding concerning the lawyer's representation of the client"). See also Rule 1.9(c)(disclosure of information pertaining to representation of former client prohibited except as permitted or required by other rules). The lack of an authorization, however, limits what can be discussed. Such conversations must be strictly limited to trial counsel's representation of the client and to the claims raised in the habeas petition. The content of documents cannot be discussed absent prior authorized disclosure.

Trial counsel, of course, is under no legal obligation to speak with habeas counsel. However, much like the voluntary disclosure of file notes, such conversations may be in the client's (and counsel's) best interest and may serve to better understand decisions made by counsel at trial. See Strickland, 466 U.S. at 691 ("inquiry into counsel's conversations with the defendant may be critical to a proper assessment of counsel's investigation decisions, just as it may be critical to a proper assessment of counsel's other litigation decisions.").

B. Appellate Counsel's File

If the habeas petition includes, or is anticipated to include, a claim of ineffective assistance of counsel on appeal, every effort should be made to obtain a copy of appellate counsel's file. The rules that pertain to obtaining a copy of trial counsel's file also apply to obtaining a copy of appellate counsel's file. The request for a copy of the file must include all transcripts in appellate counsel's possession and a copy of the briefs, appendices and record filed on appeal.

Although appellate counsel can legally withhold his or her notes, every effort should be made to persuade appellate counsel to disclose the notes, as the notes may be relevant to appellate counsel's decision not to raise and brief a particular legal issue or to choose one issue over another. Appellate counsel should be advised that appellate counsel might be asked on the witness stand about his or her decision-making and that it may be in the best interest of the petitioner (and appellate counsel) to disclose and discuss the notes now.

Even if the habeas petition does not include, or is not anticipated to include, a claim of ineffective assistance of counsel on appeal, habeas counsel should obtain from appellate counsel all transcripts in appellate counsel's possession and a copy of the briefs, appendices and record filed on appeal. Such items are still relevant and necessary to perfecting a claim of ineffective assistance of counsel at trial or to defeating any defenses the respondent may raise. <u>See</u> <u>infra</u> *T. RESPONDENT'S DEFENSES*.

C. Prior Habeas Counsel's File

If the habeas petition includes, or is anticipated to include, a claim of ineffective assistance of counsel in the prior habeas, <u>see</u> <u>Lozada v. Warden</u>, 223 Conn. 834 (1992), every effort should be made to obtain a copy of prior habeas counsel's file. This is critical to perfecting a claim that prior habeas counsel rendered ineffective assistance.

The rules that pertain to obtaining a copy of trial counsel's file also apply to obtaining a copy of prior habeas counsel's file. Counsel can again withhold his or her notes, but an attempt should be made to persuade counsel to disclose the notes, so as to conclusively litigate the issues in the case.

CHAPTER 8.

APPELLATE OPINIONS

The appellate opinion in the case must be promptly obtained and read, as it often serves as habeas counsel's initial foray into the case. Though not a substitute for a review of the trial transcript, the appellate opinion generally provides a good summary of the facts of the crime and certainly identifies some or all of the legal issues that arose at trial. Habeas counsel must also obtain the appellate briefs and appendices and the appellate record. This is especially true if a claim of ineffective assistance of appellate counsel is contemplated or certain defenses are anticipated. See infra T. *RESPONDENT'S DEFENSES*.

CHAPTER 9.

TRIAL COURT CLERK'S FILE

A. Judgment

During the process of identifying meritorious claims and amending the petition, habeas counsel should obtain a copy of the judgment, which is prepared by the trial court clerk. It will be found in the clerk's file, as well as in the appellate record. It is typically a one or two-page document. Practice Book § 23-36 provides for the filing of a copy of any portion of the clerk's file in the habeas court.

B. Other Records

During the process of identifying meritorious claims and amending the petition, habeas counsel should obtain a copy of any and all notes issued by the jury. The notes will be found in the trial court clerk's file. The notes can be helpful in establishing harmful error, in that they often reveal the jury's focus. Practice Book § 23-36 provides for the filing of a copy of any portion of the clerk's file in the habeas court.

C. Trial Exhibits

During the process of identifying meritorious claims and amending the petition, habeas counsel should obtain a copy of the trial exhibit list. Habeas counsel should also travel to the clerk's office and physically examine the exhibits introduced in evidence at trial. This ensures both the existence of the exhibits and counsel's familiarity with the exhibits. Practice Book § 23-36 provides for the filing of a copy of any portion of the clerk's file in the habeas court.

CHAPTER 10.
ORIGINAL DISCOVERY

It is vitally important that habeas counsel make every effort to determine what was and was not provided in discovery by the prosecutor to trial counsel. Proof of disclosure will undermine any testimony from trial counsel that he did not act because he did not receive, or was otherwise unaware of, certain information. Some Part A State's Attorney's Offices will attach a discovery letter to the disclosure, listing each document or item that is being provided to trial counsel. Such a letter makes the task of identifying the materials disclosed to trial counsel considerably easier. If such a letter is not in trial counsel's file, consult the State's Attorney's Office to learn that office's practice and to obtain a copy of the letter.

CHAPTER 11.
TRANSCRIPTS

A claim of ineffective assistance of counsel at trial cannot be perfected without obtaining the transcript of the trial, including jury selection and sentencing. Transcripts of suppression hearings and oral argument on pretrial motions should also be obtained by habeas counsel. If the focus of the habeas petition is a plea and sentencing, transcripts of those proceedings should obviously be obtained. The arraignment and relevant court appearance transcripts should be added to the list if jail credit is at stake. Practice Book § 23-36 provides for the filing of the transcripts in the habeas court.

If an appeal has been taken, some or all of transcripts will be in the possession of appellate counsel and can usually be obtained by supplying appellate counsel with an authorization signed by the client.

CHAPTER 12.

PRIVATE INVESTIGATION

If the habeas petition alleges that defense counsel was deficient because counsel failed to adequately investigate the facts or locate an exculpatory witness, habeas counsel must retain a private investigator to do what defense counsel did not do. This should be done without delay because the investigation may give rise to additional and unforeseen activities—things that take time. Habeas counsel cannot be left with too little time to complete the investigation, thus jeopardizing the habeas case. Further, without a private investigation the petitioner cannot satisfy Strickland's prejudice prong because he cannot show what the results would have been if defense counsel had not been negligent. See Holley v. Commissioner, 62 Conn. App. 170, 175 (2001)("The burden to demonstrate what benefit additional investigation would have revealed is on the petitioner."). The habeas case will best be served if the private investigator has a law enforcement background or prior experience conducting investigations in criminal cases. The case will also best be served if the investigator has a familiarity with the town or city where the crime occurred.

If the petitioner is without the funds to hire a private investigator, request should be made of the Office of Chief Public Defender (OCPD), 30 Trinity Street, 4th FL, Hartford, CT 06106; telephone 860-509-6400, for permission to obtain an investigator at OCPD's expense. This is true even in a case where habeas counsel is privately retained.

In addition to requesting OCPD to fund the private investigation, counsel can file a motion (ex parte and under seal if necessary) with the habeas court, seeking court authorization to employ an investigator at state expense, pursuant to the federal and state constitutions and Ake v. Oklahoma, 470 U.S. 68 (1985).

CHAPTER 13.

MENTAL STATE ASSESSMENT

If the habeas petition alleges that defense counsel was deficient because he or she failed to investigate the petitioner's mental state at the time of the crime, habeas counsel must retain a mental health expert, such as a forensic psychologist or psychiatrist, to examine the petitioner and make a reasoned determination about the petitioner's mental state at the time of the crime. Habeas counsel should also supply the expert with any informative documents, such as police reports, school records, DCF records, military records, work records, medical records and mental health records. Without the findings of a mental health expert, the petitioner cannot satisfy Strickland's prejudice prong because the petitioner cannot show what the results would have been if defense counsel had taken the appropriate steps and investigated the petitioner's mental state.

The retention of a mental health expert should be done without delay, as the assessment can take several weeks or months. Further, the assessment may reveal the need to obtain a more specialized expert, further adding to the length of the process. Thus, by promptly retaining the expert, habeas counsel ensures that the assessment will be complete well before trial and that the case will not be jeopardized.

If the petitioner is without the funds to hire a mental health expert, request should be made of the Office of Chief Public Defender (OCPD), 30 Trinity Street, 4th FL, Hartford, CT 06106; telephone 860-509-6400, for permission to obtain an expert at OCPD's expense. This is true even in a case where habeas counsel is privately retained.

In addition to requesting OCPD to fund the assessment, counsel can file a motion (ex parte and under seal if necessary) with the habeas court, seeking court authorization to employ a mental health expert at state expense, pursuant to the federal and state constitutions and Ake v. Oklahoma, 470 U.S. 68 (1985).

CHAPTER 14.
FORENSIC TESTING

If the habeas petition alleges that defense counsel was deficient because counsel failed to have certain forensic testing performed, habeas counsel must retain a qualified expert to conduct the requisite testing. This must be done without delay because the testing may take longer than anticipated or may give rise to further testing. Habeas counsel cannot be left with too little time to complete the testing, thus jeopardizing the habeas case. Further, without such testing, the petitioner cannot satisfy Strickland's prejudice prong because the petitioner cannot show what the testing would have yielded if it had been secured by defense counsel. See Aillon v. Meachum, 211 Conn. 352, 363-64 (1989)(no hair expert produced at habeas trial to demonstrate that expert testimony at original criminal trial would have been favorable).

However, before an expert is retained, habeas counsel must confirm the existence and location of the items to be tested. This will generally require habeas counsel to travel to the court clerk's office to review the trial exhibits or to travel to the police station or prosecutor's office to review other items that did not become part of the trial.

If court approval is needed to take possession of an item and to have it tested, such approval should be sought without delay via an appropriately tailored motion. The motion should cite Practice Book § 23-38; Bracy v. Gramley, 520 U.S. 899, 908-09 (1997)("[w]here specific allegations before the court show reason to believe that the petitioner may, if the facts are fully developed, be able to demonstrate that he is ... entitled to relief, it is the duty of the courts to provide the necessary facilities and procedures for an adequate inquiry")(internal quotation marks omitted; citation omitted); Giles v. Maryland, 386 U.S. 66, 74 (1967)(prosecution has a duty to disclose and/or make available any evidence that could be used in obtaining favorable evidence); and State v. Hammond, 221 Conn. 264, 292-93 (1992)(State has ethical duty, even after trial, to assist in pursuit of relevant, exculpatory evidence).

If the petitioner lacks the funds to hire a forensic expert, request should be made of the Office of Chief Public Defender (OCPD), 30 Trinity Street, 4th FL, Hartford, CT

06106; telephone 860-509-6400, for permission to obtain an expert at OCPD's expense. This is true even in a case where habeas counsel is privately retained.

In addition to requesting OCPD to fund the testing, counsel can file a motion (ex parte and under seal if necessary) with the habeas court, seeking court authorization to hire an expert at state expense, pursuant to the federal and state constitutions and Ake v. Oklahoma, 470 U.S. 68 (1985).

See infra S. *HABEAS DISCOVERY RULES* for additional guidance on this topic.

CHAPTER 15.

EXPERT WITNESSES

To the extent an expert witness is anticipated to testify at the habeas trial, habeas counsel must provide notice of the expert pursuant to Practice Book §§ 13-4 and 23-38.

A. Legal Expert

In <u>Evans v. Warden</u>, 29 Conn. App. 274, 275 (1992), the Appellate Court held "that the testimony of a legal expert is [not] required, as a matter of law, in every habeas corpus petition in order to establish ineffective assistance of counsel." <u>See also</u> <u>Id.</u> at 280-81 ("We are not persuaded that we should adopt an inflexible requirement that expert testimony must be presented in every case raising a *Strickland* inquiry. The case-by-case approach is appropriate in a situation involving ineffective assistance of counsel."). The Appellate Court noted, however, that the habeas judge may not be "cognizant of the required standard of 'reasonable competence' displayed by lawyers with ordinary training and skill in the criminal law; Strickland v. Washington, supra, 687; at the time the challenged representation is alleged to have occurred." Id. at 281-82.

Later, in Johnson v. Commissioner, 34 Conn. App. 153, cert. denied, 229 Conn. 919 (1994), the habeas court dismissed the petitioner's ineffective assistance of counsel claim, holding that without the testimony of a legal expert, the petitioner could not establish that trial counsel was deficient. The Appellate Court affirmed the decision, stating: "A trial court has broad discretion in determining whether expert testimony is need. ...In this case, because of the complexity of the issues, the habeas court determined that expert testimony was necessary for a determination of whether the trial counsel's performance was incompetent, and that, without such expert testimony, no finding as to competency could be made." (citation omitted) Id. at 158.

Thus, it could be, and often is the case, that habeas counsel must present the testimony of a legal expert to establish the "prevailing professional norms," Strickland, 466 U.S. at 688, at the time in question. The failure to do so—to establish the requisite benchmark—could prove fatal in some cases. Accordingly, a legal expert should be consulted with regard to the habeas claims and, if in agreement with their merit, presented as an expert witness at the habeas trial.

B. Other Experts

The need at the habeas trial for other expert witnesses such as physicians, psychologists, and forensic and social scientists, just to name a few, will be determined by the nature of the habeas claims and what trial counsel achieved or failed to achieve at the original criminal trial. To the extent such experts are needed, they should be consulted and retained without delay. This will ensure that they have ample time to complete the work, that they are prepared to testify, and that any and all reciprocal discovery provisions or orders have been complied with in a timely manner.

CHAPTER 16.

LEGAL RESOURCES

The following are useful resources in identifying, developing and drafting habeas corpus claims:

J. Liebman & R. Hertz, <u>Federal Habeas Corpus Practice And Procedure</u>

(7th Ed. 2015)

B. R. Means, <u>Federal Habeas Manual</u> *A Guide To Federal Habeas Corpus Litigation* (2014)

J. Burkoff & N. Burkoff, <u>Ineffective Assistance of Counsel</u> (2012 Ed.)

I.P. Robbins, <u>Habeas Corpus Checklists</u> (2015-16 Ed.)

L. Fassler, <u>Ineffective Assistance of Counsel</u> (1993, 1994)

J. Hall, Jr., <u>Professional responsibility Of The Criminal Lawyer</u> (1987)

J. Purver & L. Taylor, <u>Handling Criminal Appeals</u> (1980)

ABA Standards for Criminal Justice, Prosecution Function and Defense Function (3rd Ed. 1993)

ABA Standards for Criminal Justice, Discovery and Trial by Jury (3rd Ed. 1996)

ABA Standards for Criminal Justice, Pleas of Guilty (3rd Ed. 1999)

Connecticut Rules of Professional Conduct (West 2016)

Bruckmann, Nash & Katz, Connecticut Criminal Caselaw Handbook (1989

Colin C. Tait & Hon. Eliot D. Prescott, Tait's Handbook Of Connecticut Evidence (5th Ed. 2014)

CHAPTER 17.
MOTION FOR CONTINUANCE

A motion for continuance of the habeas case should cite Practice Book §§ 44-18, 14-11, and 14-25 and Hawk v. Olson, 326 U.S. 271, 278 (1945) ("The defendant needs counsel, and counsel needs time."); White v. Ragan, 324 U.S. 760, 764 (1945)(finding it "a denial of the accused's constitutional right to a fair trial to force him to trial with such expedition as to deprive him of the effective aid and assistance of counsel"); and Brescia v. NewJersey, 417 U.S. 921(1974)(Marshall & Brennan, JJ., dissenting from denial of cert.)("Timely appointment and opportunity for adequate preparation are absolute prerequisites for counsel to fulfill his constitutionally assigned role of seeing to it that available defenses are raised and the prosecution put to its proof."). Habeas counsel may also find State v. Day, 233 Conn. 813, 875-78 (1995) helpful on the issue of a continuance.

Any impact on the scheduling orders, <u>see</u> Practice Book § 23-35, should be addressed in the motion.

"[T]he denial of a request for a continuance is appealable." <u>Jackson v. Commissioner</u>, 227 Conn. 124, 136 (1993).

CHAPTER 18.

AMENDED PETITION

A. Petitioner's Pro Se Claims

See supra B. PRO SE HABEAS PETITIONS

B. Claims Inside & Outside the Record

The amended petition "must set forth specific grounds for the issuance of the writ including the basis for the claim of illegal confinement.... The petition for a writ of habeas corpus is essentially a pleading and, as such, it should conform generally to a complaint in a civil action.... The principle that a plaintiff may rely only upon what he has alleged is basic.... It is fundamental in our law that the right of a plaintiff to recover is limited to the allegations of his complaint.... While the habeas court has considerable discretion to frame a remedy that is commensurate with the scope of the established constitutional violations ... it does not have the discretion to look beyond the pleadings and trial evidence to decide claims not raised.... The purpose of the [petition] is to put the [respondent] on notice of the claims made, to limit the issues to be decided, and to prevent surprise." (internal citations omitted; internal quotation marks omitted) Jenkins v. Commissioner, 52 Conn. App. 385, 406, cert. denied, 249 Conn. 920 (1999); see Lebron v. Commissioner, 274 Conn. 507, 519 (2005), overruled in part on other grounds, State v. Elson, 311 Conn. 726 (2014); see also Carpenter v. Commissioner, 274 Conn. 834, 842 (2005)("As long as the pleadings provide sufficient notice of the facts claimed and the issues to be tried and do not surprise or prejudice the opposing party, we will not conclude that the complaint is insufficient to allow recovery." (internal quotation marks omitted; citations omitted)). The specific rules that govern pleadings in habeas cases are contained in Practice Book §§ 23-22 to 23-33. The rules pertaining to pleadings in civil cases also apply. See Practice Book § 10-1, et seq.

Accordingly, the amended petition should include claims inside the record, specifically, counsel's errors at trial, including the proceedings leading up to trial. The amended petition should also include counsel's errors on appeal, such as failing to adequately brief an issue or failing to supply the part of the record needed to decide an issue. The amended petition should also include claims outside the record, such as trial counsel's failure to conduct an adequate investigation of the facts, or appellate counsel's failure to recognize and brief a meritorious claim. The claims should be plead as a violation of the right to effective assistance of counsel. In appropriate cases, the claims may also be plead as a violation of a constitutional right. The same set of facts will support both counts. <u>See, e.g.</u> <u>Hernandez v. Commissioner</u>, <u>supra</u>, 82 Conn. App. 701; <u>Guadalupe v. Commissioner</u>, 68 Conn. App. 376, <u>cert. denied</u>, 260 Conn. 913 (2002). Two counts is often the prudent approach notwithstanding case law indicating that "in certain circumstances, a petitioner's claim of a constitutional violation is so inextricably bound up in the issue of the effectiveness of trial counsel, that a separate claim of a constitutional violation is not required." <u>Carpenter v. Commissioner</u>, 274 Conn. 834, 843 (2005).

Regardless of whether a claim lies inside or outside the record, habeas counsel, when amending the petition, must consult the time limitations set forth in General Statutes § 52-470(c)(d)(e)(f). Familiarity with the one-year time limitation that governs federal habeas corpus petitions is also recommended. <u>See</u> 28 U.S.C. § 2244(d)(1)(one-year statute of limitations).

C. Ineffective Assistance of Counsel (IAC)

A claim of ineffective assistance of counsel cannot be raised on direct appeal, but rather must be raised in a habeas petition. Valeriano v. Bronson, 209 Conn. 75 (1988); State v. Leecan, 198 Conn. 517, cert. denied, 476 U.S. 1184 (1986). The filing of the habeas petition, or amended petition, need not await the outcome of the appeal. See State v. Leecan, 198 Conn. at 541-42; see also Sutton v. Robinson, 6 Conn. App. 518 (1986).

The following are some of the more common claims of ineffective assistance of counsel:

a. Failure to Investigate

i. For Trial

The Sixth Amendment and Article First, § 8 require defense counsel "to investigate all surrounding circumstances of the case and to explore all avenues that may potentially lead to facts relevant to the defense of the case." Williams v. Commissioner, 100 Conn. App. 94, 102, cert. denied, 282 Conn. 914 (2007). They "impose[] on counsel a duty to investigate, because ... effective assistance must be based on professional decisions and informed legal choices can be made only after investigation of options." Strickland v. Washington, 466 U.S. 668, 680 (1984)(summarizing the holding of the Fifth Circuit); see also Siemon v. Stoughton, 184 Conn. 547, 554 (1981)(Article First, § 8 guarantees effective assistance of counsel); Id. at 557 ("Counsel must make his decisions on an informed basis."). In Siemon v. Stoughton, supra, 184 Conn. 547, the Connecticut Supreme Court held that "[c]onstitutionally adequate assistance of counsel includes competent pretrial investigation." 184 Conn. at 554 (citing State v. Clark, 170 Conn. 273, 283, cert. denied, 425 U.S. 962 (1976)). This includes "the duty ... to investigate the relevant material in the state's attorney's file." Siemon, 184 Conn. at 557.

The American Bar Association standards are informative. Standard 4-4.1 *Duty To Investigate* of ABA Standards for Criminal Justice, Defense Function (3rd Ed. 1993), provides in pertinent part: "(a) Defense counsel should conduct a prompt investigation of the circumstances of the case and to explore all avenues leading to facts relevant to the merits of the case.... The investigation should include efforts to secure information in the possession of the prosecution and law enforcement authorities. The duty to investigate exists regardless of the accused's admissions or statements to defense counsel...."

See also Id. Commentary ("Facts form the basis of effective representation.").

Guidance can also be found in the Rules of Professional Conduct. Rule 1.1 *Competence* states that "[c]ompetent representation requires the … thoroughness and preparation reasonably necessary for the representation." See also Id. Official Commentary ("The required attention and preparation are determined in part by what is at stake…."). Rule 1.3 *Diligence* holds that "[a] lawyer shall act with reasonable diligence and promptness in representing a client."

An "inadequate pretrial investigation is sufficient to constitute ineffective assistance of counsel." Siemon, 184 Conn. at 556. And the "failure to conduct an adequate investigation is not a matter of trial tactics." Id. at 557. The latter principle was reaffirmed in Ostolaza v. Warden, 26 Conn. App. 758, 765, cert. denied, 222 Conn. 906 (1992)("[t]he failure to conduct an adequate investigation cannot be excused in the penumbra of trial tactics").

However, "strategic choices made after thorough investigation of law and facts relevant to plausible options are virtually unchallengeable; and strategic choices made after less than complete investigation are reasonable precisely to the extent that reasonable professional judgments support the limitations on the investigation. In other words, counsel has a duty to make reasonable investigations or to make a reasonable decision that makes particular investigations unnecessary. In any ineffectiveness case, a particular decision not to investigate [will] be directly assessed for reasonableness in all the circumstances, applying a heavy measure of deference to counsel's judgments." Strickland, 466 U.S. at 690-91; see Gaines v. Commissioner, 306 Conn. 664, 680 (2012).

"The reasonableness of an attorney's investigative decisions often depends critically on the information supplied by his client." Williams v. Warden, 217 Conn. 419, 426 (1991). The investigative decision, however, must be evaluated in light of the information available to defense counsel from all sources and not just from the defendant. Thus, the principle that it is not deficient for defense counsel to fail to investigate a favorable witness that has not been made known to counsel by the defendant does not apply when counsel knew or should have known of the witness from other sources. See Gaines v. Commissioner, 306 Conn. at 684; see also

Skakel v. Warden, Tolland J.D., at Rockville, Docket No. CV-10-4003762 (Bishop, J.T.R), Mem. Of Dec., Oct. 23, 2013, p. 55-56.

The issue of defense counsel's failure to investigate was raised in the following habeas cases: <u>Siemon</u>, <u>supra</u>, 184 Conn. 547 (counsel ineffective for failing to investigate third-party culpability suspect); <u>Gaines</u>, 306 Conn. at 669-87 (performance deficient when investigation without explanation left two alibi witnesses undiscovered); <u>Thompson v. Commissioner</u>, 131 Conn. App. 671, 694-97 (decision not to interview and present two witnesses did not render investigation inadequate because counsel determined that testimony would contradict defense theory), <u>cert. denied</u>, 303 Conn. 902 (2011); <u>Stepney v. Commissioner</u>, 129 Conn. App. 364, 367-68 (2011) (failure to investigate and to introduce DNA report was matter of trial strategy); <u>Davis v. Warden</u>, 32 Conn. App. 296, 304-05 (decision not to investigate implausible alternative defense after proper investigation of murders and surrounding circumstances constituted reasonable professional judgment and effective assistance), <u>cert. denied</u>, 227 Conn. 924 (1993); <u>Williams v. Bronson</u>, 21 Conn. App. 260, 267-68 (1990) (counsel not ineffective for failing to memorialize in writing witness' statement at interview); <u>Chace v. Bronson</u>, 19 Conn. App. 674, 678-80 (counsel not deficient for failing to expand investigation because counsel had sufficient information to conclude that additional interviews were unnecessary), <u>cert. denied</u>, 231 Conn. 801 (1989). The foregoing list is not exhaustive.

Deficient performance stemming from counsel's failure without adequate explanation to locate a favorable witness is discussed at length in J. Burkoff & N. Burkoff, Ineffective Assistance Of Counsel (2012 Ed.), §§ 6:34 and 7:19.

ii. For Sentencing

The Sixth Amendment and Article First, § 8 also require defense counsel to investigate the defendant's character, background and history, so as to identify and present at sentencing evidence that may mitigate the punishment. See State v. Binet, 192 Conn. 618, 631 (1984)("...[t]o 'mitigate' an offense is to introduce proof which results in a 'reduction of punishment.'" (citations omitted)). The failure to do so, in whole or in part, may constitute ineffective assistance of counsel under Strickland. See Williams v. Taylor, 529 U.S. 362, 396 (2000)("obligation to conduct a thorough investigation of the defendant's background); Wiggins v. Smith, 539 U.S. 510 (2003)(counsel's failure to expand background investigation denied defendant effective assistance of counsel at sentencing); see, e.g. Porter v. McCollum, 528 U.S. 30, 31(2009)("Like the District Court, we are persuaded that it was objectively unreasonable to conclude there was no reasonable probability the sentence would have been different if the sentencing judge and jury had heard the significant mitigation evidence that Porter's counsel neither uncovered nor presented. We therefore grant the petition for certiorari in part and reverse the judgment of the Court of appeals." (original footnote omitted)).

The obligation to investigate the defendant's character, background and history for sentencing purposes does not require the same investigation in each case. See Cullen v. Pinholster, 563 U.S. 170, ____, 131 S.Ct. 1388, 1406-07 (2011)("Strickland itself rejected the notion that the same investigation will be required in every case").

In reviewing defense counsel's investigation, the habeas court will determine whether counsel conducted a reasonable background investigation or made a reasonable decision that made conducting a background investigation unnecessary. See Cullen v. Pinholster, 563 U.S. at ____, 131 S.Ct. at 1407 (quoting parenthetically Strickland, 466 U.S. at 691).

For further discussion on the deficiencies of counsel related to sentencing, see supra A. *HABEAS CORPUS JURISPRUDENCE* 1.b. *Ineffective Assistance of Counsel at Sentencing*.

b. Failure to Consult or Retain Expert

"[T]here is no per se rule that requires a trial attorney

to seek out an expert witness." (internal quotation marks omitted; citation omitted) <u>Antonio A. v. Commissioner</u>, 148 Conn. App. 825, 833, <u>cert. denied</u>, 312 Conn. 901 (2014). However, "in some cases, 'the failure to use any expert can result in a determination that a criminal defendant was denied the effective assistance of counsel.'" <u>Id.</u> (quoting <u>Peruccio v. Commissioner</u>, 107 Conn. App. 66, 76, <u>cert. denied</u>, 287 Conn. 920 (2008)). This is because "[c]riminal cases will arise where the only reasonable and available defense strategy requires consultation with experts or introduction of expert evidence...." <u>Harrington v. Richter</u>, 562 U.S. 86, 106 (2011). Thus, in such situations, defense counsel's failure to consult and/or retain a qualified expert may constitute ineffective assistance of counsel. <u>See, e.g.</u>, <u>Troedel v. Wainwright</u>, 667 F.Supp. 1456 (S.D.Fla. 1886), <u>aff'd without op.</u> 828 F.2d 670. In <u>Stephen S. v. Commissioner</u>, 134 Conn. App. 801, <u>cert. denied</u>, 304 Conn. 932 (2012), the Connecticut Appellate Court held that "cases involving child sexual abuse may, depending on the circumstances, require some pretrial investigation and consultation with experts." <u>Id.</u> at 815.

If the record reveals that trial counsel, after consultation with the expert, elected, as a matter of strategy, not to call the witness to testify, the decision is virtually unchallengeable. <u>See Antonio A. v. Commissioner</u>,

148 Conn. App. at 833-34. The only way to attack the decision is to show that the underlying strategy was fundamentally flawed and completely against the client's interests.

Related, in <u>Hinton v. Alabama</u>, 571 U.S. __, __, 134 S.Ct. 1081, 1088 (2014), the Supreme Court held that trial counsel's "failure to request additional funding in order to replace an expert he knew to be inadequate because he mistakenly believed that he had received all he could get under Alabama law constituted deficient performance."

c. Failure to Communicate or Recommend Plea Bargain

Plea bargaining is a critical stage of the criminal proceedings. <u>Hill v. Lockhart</u>, 474 U.S. 52 (1985); <u>see</u> <u>Padilla v. Kentucky</u>, 559 U.S. 356 (2010), <u>see also</u> <u>Copas v. Commissioner</u>, 234 Conn. 139, 153 (1995), <u>overruled sub silencio on other grounds</u>, <u>Washington v. Commissioner</u>, 287 Conn. 792 (2008); <u>Johnson v. Commissioner</u>, 36 Conn. App. 695 (1995). "[C]riminal defendants require effective assistance of counsel during plea negotiations." <u>Missouri v. Frye</u>, 566 U.S. __, __, 132 S.Ct. 1399, 1407-08 (2012); <u>see also</u> <u>McMann v. Richardson</u>, 397 U.S. 759, 771 (1970). Ineffective assistance of counsel claims that relate to plea bargaining are governed by <u>Strickland</u>. <u>See</u> <u>Hill v. Lockhart</u>,

474 U.S. at 57-58.

i. Failure to Communicate Plea Bargain

Multiple authorities require defense counsel to communicate to the defendant any plea bargain extended by the prosecution. See Missouri v. Frye, 566 U.S. at __, 132 S.Ct. at 1408 ("This Court now holds that, as a general rule, defense counsel has the duty to communicate formal offers from the prosecution to accept a plea on terms and conditions that may be favorable to the accused."); see also H.P.T. v. Commissioner, 127 Conn. App. 480, 483-84 (2011)(counsel must provide adequate notice of plea offer), rev'd on other grounds, 310 Conn. 606 (2013); Sanders v. Commissioner, 83 Conn. App. 543, 546-52 (counsel must "meaningfully explain" plea offer to client), cert. denied, 271 Conn. 914 (2004); see generally Practice Book §§ 39-3, 39-19 and 39-20; ABA Standards for Criminal Justice, Defense Function (3rd Ed. 1993), Standard 4-3.8 *Duty to Keep Client Informed* ("(a) Defense counsel should keep the client informed of the developments in the case...."); Standard 4-6.2 *Plea Discussions* ("(a) Defense counsel should keep the accused advised of developments arising out of plea discussions conducted with the prosecutor. (b) Defense counsel should promptly communicate and explain to the accused all significant plea proposals made by the prosecutor."); ABA Standards for Criminal Justice, Pleas of Guilty (3rd Ed. 1999), Standard 14-3.2 *Responsibilities of Defense Counsel* ("(a) Defense counsel should keep the defendant advised of developments arising out of plea discussions conducted with the prosecuting attorney, and should promptly communicate and explain to the defendant all plea offers made by the prosecuting attorney."); Rules of Professional Conduct, Rule 1.4 *Communication*.

Defense counsel's failure to communicate to the defendant a plea bargain offered by the prosecution constitutes deficient performance under Strickland. See Frye, 566 U.S. at ___, 132 S.Ct. at 1408 ("When defense counsel allowed the offer to expire without advising the defendant or allowing him to consider it, defense counsel did not render the effective assistance of counsel the Constitution requires."). Prejudice under Strickland is established when it is shown that the defendant would have accepted the plea bargain had he known about it and there is no reasonable probability the trial judge would have rejected the plea bargain or refused the defendant's plea. See Frye, 566 U.S. at ___, 132 S.Ct. at 1409-10.

ii. Failure to Recommend Plea Bargain Due to Incompetence

The Strickland standard also applies when a defendant has rejected a plea bargain due to the erroneous advice of defense counsel. Lafler v. Cooper, 566 U.S. ___, 132 S.Ct. 1376 (2012). Under the performance prong, the petitioner must establish "'that counsel's representation fell below an objective standard of reasonableness.'" Lafler v. Cooper, 566 U.S. at __, 132 S.Ct at 1384 (quoting Strickland, 466 U.S. at 688). Put differently, the petitioner must show that defense counsel's assistance was not "reasonably competent or within the range of competence displayed by lawyers with ordinary training and skill in the criminal law" and but for the erroneous advice, the petitioner would have accepted the plea bargain, thus avoiding trial and the harsher punishment which followed. See Ebron v. Commissioner, 307 Conn. 342, 351-52 (2012), cert. denied in part on other grounds sub. nom., Arnone v. Ebron, U.S. ___, 133 S.Ct. 1726 (2013); see also Myers v. Manson, 192 Conn. 383, 394 (1984); Buckley v. Warden, 177 Conn. 538, 542-43 (1979)(there must be "an interrelationship" between the ineffective assistance and the petitioner's decision); Perez v. Commissioner, 80 Conn. App. 96, 99, cert. denied, 266 Conn. 954 (2003); Baillargeon v. Commissioner, 67 Conn. App. 716, 721-22 (2002).

Under the prejudice prong, the petitioner must establish "'that there is a reasonable probability that, but for counsel's unprofessional errors, the result of the proceeding would have been different.'" Lafler, 566 U.S. at , 132 S.Ct at 1384 (quoting Strickland, 466 U.S. at 694). "In the context of pleas [the petitioner] must show the outcome of the pleas process would have been different with competent advice." Id. , 132 S.Ct at 1384. More specifically, the petitioner "must show that but for the ineffective advice of counsel there is a reasonable probability that the plea offer would have been presented to the court ..., that the court would have accepted its terms, and that the conviction or sentence, or both, under the offer's terms would have been less severe than under the judgment and sentence that in fact were imposed." Id. at ___, 132 S.Ct. at 1385; see also Ebron v. Commissioner, 307 Conn. at 351-57.

iii. Remedy

The remedies enunciated in Missouri v. Frye, supra, 566 U.S. __, 132 S.Ct. 1399, and Lafler v. Cooper, supra, 566 U.S. , 132 S.Ct. 1376, when both Strickland prongs have been met, are less than crystal clear. See Ebron, 307 Conn. at 354-56. Where the petitioner was convicted at trial of the same charge that was embodied in the plea bargain, the trial court, upon remand and after consideration of the offense and the petitioner's character, background and history, see Practice Book §§ 39-7 to 39-9 (conditional acceptance of plea bargain); Practice Book § 43-3, et seq. (PSI), can either let the sentence stand, impose the sentence contained in the plea bargain, or fix the sentence somewhere in between the two. Where the petitioner was convicted at trial of a charge more serious than that embodied in the plea bargain, the trial court, upon remand and after consideration of the offense and the petitioner's character, background and history, see Practice Book §§ 39-7 to 39-9 (conditional acceptance of plea bargain); Practice Book § 43-3, et seq. (PSI), can either accept a plea to the charge embodied in the plea bargain and sentence in accordance with the plea bargain, or refuse the plea bargain and place the case on the trial list. Lafler, 566 U.S. at ___, 132 S.Ct. at 1388-89; see also Ebron, 307 Conn. at 357-59; H.P.T. v. Commissioner, 310 Conn. 606, 611-16 (2013); McMillion v. Commissioner, 151 Conn. App. 861, 872-76 (2014).

iv. Other Failures

Practice Book § 39-3 provides that "[d]efense counsel ... shall insure that the decision to dispose of the case or to proceed to trial is ultimately made by the defendant." While clear, the provision does not indicate whether counsel is obligated to specifically recommend the acceptance or rejection of a particular plea bargain. The ABA Standards for Criminal Justice, for their part, while emphasizing that no recommendation should be made without "appropriate investigation and study of the case," see ABA Standards for Criminal Justice, Defense Function (3rd Ed. 1993), Standard 4-6.1(b); Pleas of Guilty (3rd Ed. 1999), Standard 14-3.2(b), fall short of obligating counsel in the first instance to make a recommendation.

Consequently, whether defense counsel, in fully discussing a plea bargain with the defendant, must also tell the defendant what decision to make, is a thorny issue. In Purdy v. United States, 208 F.3d 41 (2nd Cir. 2000), the Second Circuit observed that there is no "per se rule that defense counsel must always expressly advise the defendant whether to take a plea offer." Id. at 48. The Court concluded that counsel is not deficient if he or she informs the client "of the strength of the government's case against him, together with the nature of the government's plea offer, without specifically advising [the client] to take the plea." Id. Purdy was cited with approval in Edwards v. Commissioner, 87 Conn. App. 517, 523-25 (2005). There, defense counsel thoroughly discussed the plea negotiations with the defendant, expressed an opinion on what the defendant should do, but told the defendant he would have to make his own decision. The

Connecticut Appellate Court found that counsel's assistance was not deficient. Id. at 520-25. Subsequently, in Vazquez v. Commissioner, 123 Conn. App. 424 (2010), cert. denied, 302 Conn. 901 (2011), the Appellate Court made clear that there is no requirement that counsel advise the defendant to accept a plea bargain. Id. at 437. More recently, in Barlow v. Commissioner, 150 Conn. App. 781 (2014), where defense counsel was found deficient under Strickland for failing to give any advice whatsoever on the plea bargain, the Appellate Court stated: "Counsel should not make the decision for the defendant or in any way pressure the defendant to accept or reject the offer, but counsel should give the defendant his or her *professional* advice on the best course of action given the facts of the particular case and the potential total sentence exposure." Id. at 800 (emphasis in original). Barlow was distinguished on its facts in Andrews v. Commissioner, 155 Conn. App. 548, 553-55, cert. denied, 316 Conn. 911 (2015). There, the habeas record revealed that trial counsel advised the petitioner of the strengths and weaknesses of the prosecution's case, the charges the petitioner was facing, the maximum penalties if convicted at trial, and the strong likelihood of receiving a sentence in excess of the plea offer. The record further revealed that trial counsel told the petitioner that the State's case was strong and that it would be difficult for the petitioner to win. Id. at 554-55. The Appellate Court found that "[a]lthough trial counsel left the ultimate decision of whether to accept or to reject the offer to the petitioner, he provided the petitioner with adequate professional advice on the options and best course of action...." Id. at 555.

Accordingly, Connecticut law suggests, if not indicates, that while defense counsel need not tell the defendant what decision to make, counsel should discuss with the defendant the risks and benefits of a trial and the decision that appears to be in his or her best interest. This will require counsel to explain the strengths and weaknesses of the State's case, the likelihood of a conviction at trial, the potential penalties at stake, and the benefits, if any, offered by a plea bargain. The failure to do this may give rise to a claim of ineffective assistance of counsel. Strickland prejudice must be proven with regard to any such claim. See Barlow v. Commissioner, 150 Conn. App. at 802-05.

The failure to recommend an *exceptional* offer by the prosecution is ripe for collateral attack. See Barlow, 150 Conn. App. at 795 ("The cases which have found defense counsel wanting for failure to recommend acceptance of a plea offer have typically involved hopeless cases where going to trial was 'suicidal' and where the disparity between the plea offer and the potential sentence after trial was enormous."); see, e.g. Turner v. Tennessee, 664 F.Supp. 1113 (M.D.Tenn. 1987)(petitioner, who was convicted at trial and received life imprisonment, was denied effective assistance of counsel by trial counsel's failure to advise petitioner to accept the prosecution's offer of two-years jail), aff'd 858 F.2d 1201, 1204-08 (6th Cir. 1988), rev'd & remanded 492 U.S. 902 (1989), orig. op. aff'd on remand 940 F.2d 1000 (1991).

d. Failure to Move to Suppress

A motion to suppress evidence illegally obtained by the police or their agents should be made pursuant to the 4th, 5th, 6th and 14th Amendments to the United States Constitution; Article First, §§ 7, 8 and 9 of the Connecticut Constitution; General Statutes § 54-33f; and Practice Book §§ 41-1, et seq. and 41-12, et seq.

A motion to suppress statements of the defendant illegally obtained by the police or their agents should be made pursuant to the 4th, 5th, 6th and 14th Amendments to the United States Constitution; Article First, §§ 7, 8 and 9 of the Connecticut Constitution; Miranda v. Arizona, 384 U.S. 436 (1966); Wong Sun v. United States, 371 U.S. 471 (1963); General Statutes § 54-1c; and Practice Book §§ 41-1, et seq. and 41-12, et seq. See generally, Colin C. Tait & Hon. Eliot

D. Prescott, Tait's Handbook Of Connecticut Evidence, §
8.16.5(e)(5th Ed. 2014).

A motion to suppress statements of the defendant
illegally obtained by the police or their agents should also
be made on evidentiary grounds, specifically, that said
statements are irrelevant and/or unreliable, and/or that
the prejudice to the defendant from their admission
outweighs the probative value to the State. See Code of
Evidence, §§ 4-1 to 4-3 and 8-3; see also Perry v. New
Hampshire, 565 U.S. __, __, 132 S.Ct. 716, 729 (2012)("State
and federal rules of evidence ... permit trial judges to
exclude relevant evidence if its probative value is
substantially outweighed by its prejudicial impact or
potential for misleading the jury."); State v. Rinaldi, 220
Conn. 345, 356 (1991)(trial judge has discretion to exclude
evidence if its probative value is outweighed by its
potential for prejudice); State v. Pappas, 256 Conn. 854,
888 (2001)(articulating the countervailing factors that may
militate against the admission of probative evidence); see
generally, Colin C. Tait & Hon. Eliot D. Prescott, Tait's
Handbook Of Connecticut Evidence, §§ 4.7.2, 8.16.2 (5th Ed.
2014).

Accordingly, the failure to move to suppress evidence
or statements may constitute ineffective assistance of
counsel. The Sixth Amendment and Article First, § 8

guarantee the effective assistance of counsel. Strickland v. Washington, 466 U.S. 668 (1984); Siemon v. Stoughton, 184 Conn. 547, 554 (1981)(Article First, § 8 guarantees effective assistance of counsel). Such assistance includes, but is not limited to, the filing of pretrial motions necessary to protect the defendant's rights and to ensure a fair trial. See ABA Standards for Criminal Justice, Defense Function (3rd Ed. 1993), Standard 4-3.6 *Prompt Action to Protect the Accused* ("Many important rights of the accused can be protected and preserved only by prompt legal action. ... Defense counsel should consider all procedural steps which in good faith may be taken, including ... moving to suppress illegally obtained evidence...."); see also Rules of Professional Conduct, Rule 1.3 *Diligence* ("A lawyer shall act with reasonable diligence and promptness in representing a client.").

Also, when motions to suppress are filed, defense counsel has an obligation to ensure that such "motions, statements of grounds, argument and discussion, the ruling of the court, and the reasons given by the court for its ruling, [are] all ... made a part of the record." ABA Standards for Criminal Justice, Discovery and Trial by Jury (3rd Ed. 1996), Standard 15-3.6 *Method of Making and Ruling on Motions and Objections*; see also Practice Book §§ 5-2, 5-5, 5-6, 41-1 to 41-7, 41-12, et seq., 60-5; General Statutes §

52-208. Without an adequate record, even <u>Golding</u> review on appeal may be unattainable. <u>See</u> <u>State v. Aloi</u>, 86 Conn. App. 363, 378 (2004)("claims [must] be made at trial in order to be reviewed on appeal"), <u>rev'd on other grounds</u>, 280 Conn. 824 (2007); <u>State v. Cosby</u>, 6 Conn. App. 164, 173 (1986)(same); <u>State v. Golding</u>, 213 Conn. 233, 239-40 (1989)(defendant can prevail on constitutional claim not preserved at trial only if, among other things, record is adequate to review the alleged error); <u>see generally</u> J. Purver & L. Taylor, <u>Handling Criminal Appeals</u>, § 35, p.63 (1980)("It is ... the obligation of trial counsel, whether anticipating the possibility of being appellate counsel or not, to make sure that everything of significance that occurs during any portion of the lower court proceedings (pre-trial motions, trial, sentencing) be entered as fully and accurately as possible in the record. This cannot be over-emphasized: *appellate counsel can achieve no more than the trial record permits*." (Emphasis in original)).

If counsel's failure to move to suppress evidence or statements is motivated by a sound trial strategy, counsel has not rendered ineffective assistance. <u>See</u> <u>Williams v. Bronson</u>, 21 Conn. App. 260, 262-68 (1990).

e. Failure to Competently Select Jurors

The Sixth and Fourteenth Amendments and Article

First, § 8, as amended, guarantee a trial before an impartial jury. See Duncan v. Louisiana, 391 U.S. 145, 147-58 (1968)(6th Amendment guarantee of trial by jury made applicable to the states); Morgan v. Illinois, 504 U.S. 719, 726 (1992)(14th Amendment Due Process Clause "independently require[s] the impartiality of any jury empanelled to try the cause"); Turner v. Louisiana, 379 U.S. 466, 471-73 (1965)(impartial jury required by 14th Amendment Due Process Clause); Irwin v. Dowd, 366 U.S. 717, 722-23 (1961)(same); see also State v. Ross, 269 Conn. 213, 228 (2004).

The Sixth Amendment and Article First, § 8 also guarantee effective assistance of counsel. Strickland v. Washington, 466 U.S. 668 (1984); Siemon v. Stoughton, 184 Conn. 547, 554 (1981)(Article First, Section 8 guarantees effective assistance of counsel). This guarantee embraces jury selection, which is a critical stage of the proceedings. Competent representation at jury selection is further required by Standard 4-7.2(a) of the ABA Standards for Criminal Justice, Defense Function (3rd Ed. 1993), which states that "[d]efense counsel should prepare himself or herself prior to trial to discharge effectively his or her function in the selection of the jury, including the raising of any appropriate issues concerning the method by which the panel was selected and the exercise of both challenges for cause and peremptory challenges." The Rules of Professional Conduct lend still further support that competent representation is required at jury selection. See Rules of Professional Conduct, Rule 1.1 *Competence* ("A lawyer shall provide competent representation to a client. Competent representation requires the legal knowledge, skill, thoroughness and preparation reasonably necessary for the representation.").

An impartial jury is achieved by, among other things, excusing for cause any potential juror who demonstrates bias or an inability to be fair and impartial. It is the responsibility of counsel to move that such venire person be excused for cause pursuant to 1) the Sixth and Fourteenth Amendments which guarantee a fair trial by an impartial jury, 2) the Connecticut Constitution, Article First, § 8, as amended by Articles XVII and XXIX of the amendments, which guarantees the right to "trial by impartial jury" and the correlative right to challenge prospective jurors for cause, 3) General Statutes § 54-82f which requires that any juror "unable to render a fair and impartial verdict" be excused from service, 4) Practice Book § 42-5 which holds that a person is "disqualified to serve as a juror if such person is found by the judicial authority to exhibit any quality which will impair that person's capacity to serve," 5) Practice Book § 42-11 which holds that the "judicial authority may excuse any prospective juror for cause," and 6) Practice Book § 42-12 which states that "any juror ... unable to render a fair and impartial verdict ... shall be excused by the judicial authority ...."

Counsel's failure to move for cause or to otherwise exercise the degree of judgment and skill required to select an impartial jury constitutes deficient performance. See Skakel v. Warden, Tolland J.D., at Rockville, Docket No. CV-10-4003762 (Bishop, J.T.R), Mem. of Dec., Oct. 23, 2013, pp. 88-94, 127-30 (finding trial counsel's selection of an arguably biased juror constitutionally deficient under Strickland). In some instances the deficiency may result in structural error and per se prejudice. See Neder v. United States, 527 U.S. 1, 8 (1999)(the presence of a biased decisionmaker is structural error "subject to automatic reversal"); see also Edwards v. Balisok, 520 U.S. 641, 647 (1997)("A criminal defendant tried by a partial judge is entitled to have his conviction set aside, no matter how strong the evidence against him"). But even if the error is not considered structural, it still can and should be argued that the presence of infected jurors undermines confidence in the verdict. See Virgil v. Dretke, 446 F.3d 598, 614 (5th Cir. 2006)("Expressed in Strickland terms, the deficient performance of counsel denied [the defendant] an impartial jury, leaving him with one that could not constitutionally convict, perforce establishing Strickland prejudice with its focus upon reliability.").

f. Failure to Object

Defense counsel is obligated to object at trial to inadmissible evidence or an improper examination, unless there is a strategic reason not to object. See Practice Book §§ 5-2, 5-5, 5-6, 41-1 to 41-7, 41-12, et seq., 42-15, 60-5; see also General Statutes § 52-208; see generally Colin C. Tait & Hon. Eliot D. Prescott, Tait's Handbook Of Connecticut Evidence, § 1.30, et seq. (5th Ed. 2014). The failure to object may constitute ineffective assistance of counsel. See generally J. Hall, Jr., Professional responsibility Of The Criminal Lawyer (1987), § 4.23 ("Counsel's failure to object to evidence that is clearly inadmissible and prejudicial can be ineffective assistance."); but see Levine v. Manson, 195 Conn. 636, 648 (1985)("[t]he decision of a trial lawyer not to make an objection is a matter of trial tactics, not evidence of incompetency" (internal quotation marks omitted; citation omitted)).

An objection to anticipated improper and prejudicial evidence can also be made before trial by filing a motion in limine under Practice Book § 42-15. "A motion in limine `in a broad sense [refers] to any motion, whether made before or during trial, to exclude anticipated prejudicial evidence before the evidence is actually offered." State v. Smith, 212 Conn. 593, 611 (1989) (quoting State v. Harrell, 199 Conn. 255, 259 n. 4 (1986)(quoting in turn Luce v. United States, 469 U.S. 38, 40 n. 2 (1984))); see, e.g., State v. Smith, 212 Conn. at 611 ("defendant should have followed the common practice of filing a motion in limine to prevent any witness from referring to his prior trial").

Each occasion where counsel fails to object at trial or move in limine should be pled as a claim, or subpart of a claim, of deficient performance under Strickland. Further, the cumulative failures should be pled as a claim of deficient performance under Strickland, notwithstanding the fact that they may not be of constitutional magnitude. See Bourjaily v. United States, 483 U.S. 171, 179-80 (1987)(" [I]ndividual pieces of evidence, insufficient in themselves to prove a point, may in cumulation prove it. The sum of an evidentiary presentation may well be greater than its constituent parts.").

g. Failure to Adequately Cross-Examine and Impeach

Trial counsel's failure to adequately cross-examine or impeach a witness may constitute ineffective assistance of counsel. See J. Hall, Jr., Professional responsibility Of The Criminal Lawyer (1987), § 4.24 ("... if defense counsel possesses substantial impeachment evidence but fails to introduce it either through cross-examination or otherwise, or because he was not paying attention, ineffectiveness is shown if it is reasonably possible that the witness' testimony affected the conviction."). The failure, however, will have to be so serious that it overcomes the presumption that the examination was a product of sound trial strategy. See Antonio A. v. Commissioner, 148 Conn. App. 825, 832 ("An attorney's line of questioning on examination of a witness clearly is tactical in nature. [As such, this] court will, not in hindsight, second-guess counsel's trial strategy." (internal quotation marks omitted; citation omitted)), cert. denied, 312 Conn. 901 (2014). Strickland prejudice must also be established.

Each instance of failing to adequately cross-examine or impeach at trial should be pled as a claim, or subpart of a claim, of ineffective assistance of counsel. Further, the cumulative failures should be pled as a claim of ineffective assistance of counsel, notwithstanding the fact that they may not be of constitutional magnitude. See Bourjaily v. United States, 483 U.S. 171, 179-80 (1987)(" [I]ndividual pieces of evidence, insufficient in themselves to prove a point, may in cumulation prove it. The sum of an evidentiary presentation may well be greater than its constituent parts.").

h. Failure to Call Witness

"The failure of defense counsel to call a potential defense witness does not constitute ineffective assistance of counsel unless there is some showing that the testimony would have been helpful in establishing the asserted defense. Defense counsel will be deemed ineffective only when it is shown that a defendant has informed his attorney of the existence of the witness and that the attorney, without a reasonable investigation and without adequate explanation, failed to call the witness at trial. The reasonableness of an investigation must be evaluated not through hindsight but from the perspective of the attorney when he was conducting it." State v. Talton, 197 Conn. 280, 297-98 (1985); accord Gaines v. Commissioner, 306 Conn. 664, 680-81, 684 (2012); see also Eze v. Senkowski, 321 F.3d 110, 129 (2nd Cir. 2003)("the decision not to call a witness must be grounded in some strategy that advances the client's interests"). Logic dictates that scrutiny of counsel's decision not to call a witness should not be limited to those instances where the defendant informed counsel of the witness' existence, but should also include those instances where counsel learned of the witness through other sources, such as the State's pretrial disclosures or private investigation interviews of other witnesses.

Additionally, "an error on the part of counsel in failing to call a witness cannot be considered prejudicial, as affecting the outcome of the trial, when the evidence the witness would have given would have been cumulative." Chace v. Bronson, 19 Conn. App. 674, 681, cert. denied, 231 Conn. 801 (1989).

Defense counsel's failure to call a witness at trial was found to be deficient under Strickland in the following habeas cases: Bryant v. Commissioner, 290 Conn. 502, 509-18 (performance deficient when counsel without adequate explanation failed to present witnesses whose testimony supported third party culpability defense and undercut State's evidence), cert. denied sub nom., Murphy v. Bryant, 558 U.S. 938 (2009); Vasquez v. Commissioner, 107 Conn. App. 181, 185 (2008)(performance deficient when counsel without adequate explanation failed to present alibi witnesses); Siano v. Warden, 31 Conn. App. 94, 100-05 (performance deficient when counsel without adequate explanation failed to present physician as lone neutral witness to testify that defendant was incapable of committing crime due to injury), cert denied, 226 Conn. 910 (1993).

Defense counsel's failure to call a witness at trial was found not to be deficient under Strickland in the following habeas cases: Mozell v. Commissioner, 291 Conn. 62, 79

(2009)(decision not to present witness consistent with theory of defense); Thompson v. Commissioner, 131 Conn. App. 671, 694-97 (decision not to interview and present two witnesses did not render investigation inadequate because counsel determined that testimony would contradict defense theory), cert. denied, 303 Conn. 902 (2011); Stepney v. Commissioner, 129 Conn. App. 364, 367-68 (2011) (failure to investigate and to introduce DNA report was matter of trial strategy), cert. denied, 315 Conn. 907 (2014); State v. Gay, 108 Conn. App. 211, 218-19 (decision not to call victim at trial not ineffective because counsel believed victim would be uncooperative and potentially harmful to defense case), cert. denied, 288 Conn. 913 (2008); Chace v. Bronson, 19 Conn. App. at 680-82 (decision not to call witness at trial not ineffective because testimony might have been damaging).

Noteworthy cases outside Connecticut include Harris v. Reed, 894 F.2d 871 (7th Cir. 1990)(trial counsel's decision not to interview and call at trial two witnesses who identified a different perpetrator running from the homicide scene because he believed that the State's case was weak, that he had successfully impeached the key witness, and that the jury would deliberate for only a short time and find for the defendant was not reasonably competent and undermined the verdict).

Deficient performance stemming from counsel's failure without adequate explanation to present a favorable witness at trial is discussed in J. Burkoff & N. Burkoff, Ineffective Assistance Of Counsel (2012 Ed.), §§ 6:34 and 7:19.

i. Incompetent Expert

In Summerville v. Warden, 229 Conn. 397 (1994), the Connecticut Supreme Court declined to consider the certified question of whether an expert's negligence may be imputed to trial counsel and thus serve as a basis for ineffective assistance of counsel. Id. at 398-418. Other courts, however, have held that the failure to spend adequate time with a defense expert before trial can constitute ineffective assistance of counsel. See, e.g., Tiller v. United States, 419 A.2d 970 (D.C. App. 1980). Further, the failure to provide the complete records to the expert, thus weakening the expert's opinion, can constitute ineffective assistance of counsel. See, e.g. Hill v. Lockhart, 824 F.Supp. 1327 (E.D.Ark. 1993), rev'd on other grounds, 28 F.3d 832 (8th Cir. 1994).

Additional cases to consult include Richey v. Mitchell, 395 F.3d 660, 682-88 (6th Cir. 2005) and Bloom v. Calderon, 132 F.3d 1267 (9th Cir. 1997), cert. denied, 523 U.S. 1145 (1998).

Somewhat related to this area is Maryland v. Kulbicki, 577 U.S. ___ (2015), 2015 WL 5774453, where the Supreme Court held that trial counsel's failure to recognize or attack bad science before it is known to be bad does not constitute ineffectiveness.

j. Defendant's Right or Failure to Testify

Strickland's two-prong inquiry applies to a claim concerning any exercise of the defendant's right to testify. See Commissioner v. Rodriguez, 222 Conn. 469, 476 (1992)("claims that the defendant's right to testify was violated by defense counsel is [through] a claim of ineffective assistance of counsel [pursuant to] Strickland"); see also Ostolaza v. Warden, 26 Conn. App. 758, 764, cert. denied, 222 Conn. 906 (1992). Habeas counsel should also consult General Statutes § 54-84.

k. Failure to Object to Improper Summation

The federal and state constitutional guarantee of effective assistance of counsel applies to closing argument, which, as part of the trial, is a critical stage of the proceedings. Cf. Herring v. New York, 422 U.S. 853, 859 (1975)(the closing argument of the defense is a basic element of the adversary process and, thus, is constitutionally protected under the Sixth and Fourteenth

Amendments).

Closing argument—whether by the State or defense—must be limited to the facts in evidence, including appropriate inferences drawn the facts, and the application of the facts to the law of the case. Consequently, it is improper for counsel to misstate the facts, attribute testimony to a witness that was not provided, or refer to evidence outside the record. The rule is supported by the case law and various standards. See State v. Maguire, 310 Conn. 535, 552-55 (2013); State v. Skakel, 276 Conn. 663, 744-47, cert. denied, 549 U.S. 1030 (2006); ABA Standards For Criminal Justice, Prosecution Function (3rd Ed. 1993), Standard 3-5.8 *Argument to the Jury* ("prosecutor should not intentionally misstate the evidence or mislead the jury"); Standard 3-5.9 *Facts outside the Record* ("prosecutor should not intentionally refer to or argue on the basis of facts outside the record"); Defense Function (3rd Ed. 1993), Standard 4-7.7 *Arguments to the Jury* ("Defense counsel should not intentionally misstate the evidence or mislead the jury as to inferences it may draw."); Standard 4-7.8 *Facts Outside the Record* ("counsel should not intentionally refer to or argue on the basis of facts outside the record"); ABA Standards For Criminal Justice, Discovery and Trial by Jury (3rd Ed. 1996), Standard 15-3.4 *Opening Statement and Closing Argument,*

Commentary p. 201 ("Counsel must confine the [closing] argument to facts introduced in evidence through testimony of witnesses or other admitted exhibits, facts of common knowledge, and logical inferences based on evidence. To refer to facts not in the record, to misstate evidence, or to attribute to a witness testimony that was not given is improper.").

It is also improper for the prosecutor and defense counsel to strike at the emotions of the jury, to express personal opinions, and to denigrate the opposing party or his case. This rule is likewise supported by the case law and various standards. See State v. Maguire, 310 Conn. at 552-55; State v. Skakel, 276 Conn. at 744-47; ABA Standards For Criminal Justice, Prosecution Function (3rd Ed. 1993), Standard 3-5.8 *Argument to the Jury* ("prosecutor should not express his or her personal belief or opinion as to the truth or falsity of any testimony or evidence or the guilt of the defendant" or "make arguments calculated to appeal to the prejudices of the jury"); Defense Function (3rd Ed. 1993), Standard 4-7.7 *Arguments to the Jury* ("counsel should not express a personal belief or opinion in his or her client's innocence or personal belief or opinion in the truth or falsity of any testimony or evidence" or "make arguments calculated to appeal to the prejudices of the jury"); ABA Standards for Criminal Justice, Discovery and Trial by Jury

(3rd Ed. 1996), Standard 15-3.4 *Opening Statement and Closing Argument*, Commentary p. 202-03 ("It is improper for counsel to include remarks in ... closing argument that are not relevant to the facts and issues of the case. In addition to diverting the jury's attention from the merits of the case, such remarks can be highly prejudicial. Impermissible comments include: ... d. Emotional appeals to the jurors for sympathy or vengeance, to create fear for their personal safety.... f. Personal remarks or opinions regarding the credibility of evidence presented, or what the outcome of the case should be."); Rules Of Professional Conduct, Rule 3.4 *Fairness to Opposing Party and Counsel* ("A lawyer shall not ... [i]n trial, allude to any matter that the lawyer does not reasonably believe is relevant or that will not be supported by admissible evidence, assert personal knowledge of facts in issue except when testifying as a witness, or state a personal opinion as to the justness of a cause, the credibility of a witness, ... or the guilt or innocence of an accused").

An impermissible closing argument by the prosecution can impact the jury's decision-making and, hence, the fairness of the trial, thus requiring reversal. See State v. Ancona, 270 Conn. 568, 593-94 (2004) ("[P]rosecutorial misconduct of a constitutional magnitude can occur in the course of closing arguments...." (citation omitted)); State v.

Stevenson, 269 Conn. 563, 571 (2004)("touchstone of due process analysis in cases of alleged prosecutorial misconduct is the fairness of the trial").

A two-step analysis is used to decide claims of prosecutorial misconduct in summation. "The two steps are separate and distinct: (1) whether misconduct occurred in the first instance; and (2) whether that misconduct deprived a defendant of his due process right to a fair trial." (citation omitted; internal quotation marks omitted) State v. Stevenson, 269 Conn. at 572; accord Maguire, 310 Conn. at 552. The second step, assuming it is reached, requires the reviewing court to apply the factors set forth in State v. Williams, 204 Conn. 523, 540 (1987). See Stevenson, 269 Conn. at 572-75 (apply Williams factors, not Golding test, where prosecutorial misconduct claim is unpreserved); see also State v. Ancona, 270 Conn. at 595-96. The factors include "the extent to which the misconduct was invited by defense conduct or argument ... the severity of the misconduct ... the frequency of the misconduct ... the centrality of the misconduct to the critical issues in the case ... the strength of the curative measures adopted ... and the strength of the state's case...." Stevenson, 269 Conn. at 573 (quoting State v. Williams, 204 Conn. at 540)); see Maguire, 310 Conn. at 560. In applying the factors, "all incidents of misconduct must be viewed in relation to one another and within the context of the entire trial." Id. at 574.

Accordingly, counsel has a duty to object to any impermissible closing argument made by the prosecution, because such argument undermines the fairness of the trial and the reliability of the verdict. See State v. Ceballos, 266 Conn. 364, 414 (2003)(It is the "responsibility of defense counsel ... to object to perceived prosecutorial improprieties as they occur at trial...."). In addition to an objection, counsel should consider moving for a mistrial pursuant to Practice Book § 42-43. If the motion is denied, counsel should consider requesting a curative instruction. Counsel should also consider moving the Court for an additional opportunity to address the jury pursuant to Practice Book § 42-35 or the Court's inherent authority. See, e.g. State v. Weinberg, 215 Conn. 231, 246-51 (1990)(court permitted defendant a second opportunity to address the jury to defuse risk of prejudice stemming from inappropriate spectator conduct).

Any failure to object or seek other measures may undermine the defendant's claim on appeal. See Maguire, 310 Conn. at 560-61 ("[T]he determination of whether a new trial or proceeding is warranted depends, in part, on whether defense counsel has made a timely objection to any [incident] of the prosecutor's improper [conduct].

When defense counsel does not object, request a curative instruction or move for a mistrial, he presumably does not view the alleged impropriety as prejudicial enough to jeopardize seriously the defendant's right to a fair trial.")(quoting Stevenson, 269 Conn. at 573).

Consequently, counsel's failure to object (or to seek other measures) to improper closing argument by the prosecution will, in an appropriate case, constitute deficient performance under the Strickland standard. See generally J. Burkoff & N. Burkoff, Ineffective Assistance Of Counsel (2012 Ed.), § 7:41. Accordingly, a timely objection (and, where appropriate, a request for other measures) should be made, as the failure to do so will rarely be deemed sound trial strategy.

I. Failure to Give Competent Summation

In Herring v. New York, 422 U.S. 853 (1975), the Supreme Court stated:

> It can hardly be questioned that closing argument serves to sharpen and clarify the issues for resolution by the trier of fact in a criminal case. For it is only after all the evidence is in that counsel for the parties are in a position to present their respective versions of the case as a whole. Only then can they are the inferences

to be drawn from all the testimony, and point out the weaknesses of their adversaries' positions. And, for the defense, closing argument is the last clear chance to persuade the trier of fact that there may be reasonable doubt of the defendant's guilt. See In re Winship, 397 U.S. 358.

The very premise of our adversary system of criminal justice is that partisan advocacy on both sides of a case will best promote the ultimate objection that the guilty be convicted and the innocent go free. In a criminal trial, which is, in the end, basically a factfinding process, no aspect of such advocacy could be more important than the opportunity finally to marshal the evidence for each side before submission of the case to judgment.

Id. at 862. Thus, a competent summation is critical to the outcome of the case.

In Skakel v. Warden, Tolland J.D., at Rockville, Docket No. CV-10-4003762 (Bishop, J.T.R), the habeas court found trial counsel's summation constitutionally deficient, stating

[counsel's] closing argument was both inadequate and improper. His argument was, in the main, an unfocused running commentary on the state's evidence. Failing

even to mention the notion of reasonable doubt or to put the claim of third party culpability against Littleton into context, [counsel's] argument did not provide the jury with any template for decision making.

Mem. of Dec., Oct. 23, 2013, p. 127-28, 130.

Cases that discuss an incompetent summation include Fair v. Warden, 211 Conn. 398, 401, 410-11 (1989)(statement during summation that "there was not much question on the robbery charge," even if constitutionally deficient, did not result in prejudice); United States v. Hammonds, 425 F.2d 597, 600-04 (D.C. Cir. 1970)(counsel's "omissions and errors, and particularly the futile closing argument" established ineffective assistance); Matthews v. United States, 449 F.2d 985, 987-88 (D.C. Cir. 1971)("casual summation" constitutionally deficient but no prejudice); Cowgill v. Zimmerman, 667 F.Supp. 1083, 1086-87 (E.D.Pa. 1987)(referring to defendant as "wise ass" and "son of a bitch" in closing argument constituted constitutional deficiency under Strickland, but no prejudice); Quartararo v. Fogg, 679 F.Supp. 212, 237-53 (E.D.N.Y. 1988)(closing argument constitutionally deficient and prejudice resulted under Strickland), aff'd, 849 F.2d 1467 (2nd Cir. 1988); United States ex rel. Kubat v. Thieret, 679 F.Supp. 788, 812 (N.D.Ill.

1988)(ineffectiveness found and death sentence reversed due in part to "counsel's closing argument—a rambling, incoherent discourse that was more likely to confuse than to persuade the jury"), aff'd, 867 F.2d 351 (7th Cir. 1989); and Mathis v. Zant, 704 F.Supp. 1062 (N.D.Ga. 1989)(ineffectiveness found and death sentence reversed due in part to constitutionally deficient closing argument and prejudice).

Accordingly, an incompetent summation can and should be alleged as a claim of ineffective assistance of counsel in the habeas petition.

m. Failure to File Request to Charge or to Take Exceptions

Proposed jury instructions must be in writing, see Practice Book § 42-16, et seq., and should be filed by trial counsel pursuant to the 5th, 6th, 8th and 14th Amendments to the United States Constitution; Article First, §§ 8, 9 and 19 of the Connecticut Constitution; State v. Ortiz, 252 Conn. 533, 560-61 (2000)("a defendant is entitled to have the jury correctly and adequately instructed on the pertinent principles of substantive law"); and State v. Casey, 201 Conn. 174, 178 (1986)("A request to charge which is relevant to the issues of the case and which is an accurate statement of the law must be given."). Exceptions, preferably in writing, to the Court's anticipated charge, as well as objections to the prosecution's proposed instructions, are also required. See Practice Book § 42-16, et seq.; State v. Kitchens, 299 Conn. 447, 452-500 (2011)(underscoring the need to file a written request to charge and to object or take exception to perceived instructional flaws); see also State v. Darryl W., 303 Conn. 353, 370 (2012) (must file request to charge or take exception to the charge); State v. Paige, 304 Conn. 426, 442 (2012)(same). All objections and exceptions should be placed on the record to ensure that the Court is aware of the defendant's position and that there is an adequate record for appellate review. See Practice Book § 42-19 (requiring the charge conference to be on the record).

The failure to file proposed jury instructions may deprive the jury and, hence, the defendant of a principle of law relevant to the outcome of the case and may foreclose review of the matter on appeal. In appropriate cases, the failure to file proposed jury instructions or to object or except to instructions given, will constitute deficient performance under Strickland, as there can be no sound trial strategy for such failure. See generally J. Burkoff & N. Burkoff, Ineffective Assistance Of Counsel (2012 Ed.), § 7:46.

As to lesser-included-offenses, "counsel's failure to request a lesser included offense instruction does not necessarily deprive a defendant of reasonably effective assistance of counsel. ... It may be sound trial strategy not to request a lesser included offense instruction, hoping that the jury will simply return a not guilty verdict." (citations omitted) Fair v. Warden, 211 Conn. 398, 404 (1989); see Reeves v. Commissioner, 119 Conn. App. 852, 862, cert. denied, 962 Conn. 906 (2010). However, there have been occasions when the failure was found to be deficient. See, e.g. Chace v. Bronson, 19 Conn. App. 674, 676, 681-85 (where defendant was charged and convicted of murder, counsel was deficient under Strickland for failing to request an instruction on second-degree manslaughter, as a lesser-included-offense of murder, but such failure did not prejudice the defendant), cert. denied, 213 Conn. 801 (1989).

n. Failure to Preserve Issue For Appeal

Trial counsel's failure to preserve issues for appeal may constitute ineffective assistance of counsel. Defense counsel has an obligation to raise and preserve issues for appellate review, so as to protect the defendant's rights. See State v. Evans, 165 Conn. 61, 64-66 (1973); State v. Golding, 213 Conn. 233 (1989); State v. Elson, 311 Conn.

726 (2014); In Re Yasiel R., 317 Conn. 773 (2015); see also State v. Aloi, 86 Conn. App. 363, 378 (2004)("claims [must] be made at trial in order to be reviewed on appeal"), rev'd on other grounds, 280 Conn. 824 (2007); State v. Cosby, 6 Conn. App. 164, 173 (1986)(same); Practice Book §§ 5-2, 5-5, 5-6, 41-1, et seq., 41-12, et seq., 42-53, 42-54 and 60-5; General Statutes § 52-208; see also ABA Standards for Criminal Justice, Defense Function (3rd Ed. 1993), Standard 4-7.9 *Posttrial Motions* ("Defense counsel's responsibility includes presenting appropriate posttrial motions to protect the defendant's rights."); J. Purver & L. Taylor, Handling Criminal Appeals, § 35, p. 63 (1980)("It is ... the obligation of trial counsel, whether anticipating the possibility of being appellate counsel or not, to make sure that everything of significance that occurs during any portion of the lower court proceedings (pre-trial motions, trial, sentencing) be entered as fully and accurately as possible in the record. This cannot be over-emphasized: *appellate counsel can achieve no more than the trial record permits.*" (emphasis in original)).

D. Other Legal Claims

a. Conflict of Interest

An adjunct to the right to effective assistance of counsel is the right to be represented by an attorney who is free of any conflict of interest. See Wood v. Georgia, 450 U.S. 261, 271 (1981); Cuyler v. Sullivan, 446 U.S. 335, 345-50 (1980); Glasser v. United States, 315 U.S. 60, 70 (1942); State v. Drakeford, 261 Conn. 420, 427 (2002); Phillips v. Warden, 220 Conn. 112, 132 (1991); State v. Williams, 203 Conn. 159, 167 (1987); State v. Martin, 201 Conn. 74, 78 (1986). This right stems from the "fundamental principle ... that an attorney owes an overarching duty of undivided loyalty to [the] client." Phillips v. Warden, 220 Conn. at 136; see also ABA Standards for Criminal Justice, Defense Function (3rd Ed. 1993), Standard 4-3.5 *Conflicts of Interest*, Commentary ("The professional judgment of a lawyer should be exercised, within the bounds of the law, solely for the benefit of his or her client and free of any compromising influences and loyalties.").

Standard 4-3.5 sets forth the different types of conflicts and should be consulted in identifying, drafting and litigating a conflict of interest claim. The Rules of Professional Conduct also devote considerable attention to conflicts of interest. See Rules 1.7, 1.8, 1.9, 1.10 and 1.11. They should likewise be consulted when a conflict of interest claim is being considered for inclusion in the habeas petition.

"In a case of a claimed [actual] conflict of interest ... in order to establish a violation of the sixth amendment the [petitioner] has a two-pronged task. He must establish (1) that counsel actively represented conflicting interests and (2) that an actual conflict of interest adversely affected his lawyer's performance." (internal quotation marks omitted) Santiago v. Commissioner, 87 Conn. App. 568, 583, cert. denied, 273 Conn. 930 (2005). "To demonstrate an actual conflict of interest, the petitioner must be able to point to specific instances in the record which suggest impairment or compromise of his interests for the benefit of another party.... A mere theoretical division of loyalties is not enough." (internal quotation marks omitted) Id. at 584. "Once a petitioner has established that there is an actual conflict, he must show that a lapse of representation ... resulted from the conflict." (internal quotation marks omitted) Id.

When the defendant is denied knowledge of his or her attorney's conflict of interest, structural error results because it is impossible to say how the proceedings were affected. See State v. Lopez, 271 Conn. 724, 736-38 (2004).

b. Brady

Prior to trial, the State is required to disclose exculpatory evidence material to guilt or punishment, including impeachment evidence, in its possession (or the possession of its agents), to defense counsel pursuant to Brady v. Maryland, 373 U.S. 83 (1963), General Statutes § 54-86c(a)(c), and Practice Book § 40-11(a)(1). See Strickler v. Greene, 527 U.S. 263 (1999) (impeachment evidence is favorable under Brady); Kyles v. Whitley, 514 U.S. 419, 437 (1995)("[T]he individual prosecutor has a duty to learn of any favorable evidence known to the others acting on the [State's] behalf in the case, including the police.")

When the habeas claim is that the State failed to disclose exculpatory evidence in violation of Brady v. Maryland, the law is clear that the petitioner has a dual burden of proving the existence of the violation and, if so, that the undisclosed information is material. Brady, supra, 373 U.S. 83. In demonstrating a Brady violation, a defendant is not limited to showing that the undisclosed information is exculpatory; rather a defendant need only demonstrate that the undisclosed information is helpful to the defense. See Lapointe v. Commissioner, 316 Conn. 225 (2015)(Brady violation found because detective's undisclosed notes were exculpatory in that they supported alibi). For example, under Brady, the State would be required to disclose information that a witness has a financial interest in testifying for the State, or that a witness anticipated a favorable plea bargain in return for being a prosecution witness. See Cone v. Bell, 556 U.S. 449 (2009); Banks v. Dretke, 540 U.S. 668 (2004); see also Adams v. Commissioner, 309 Conn. 359 (2013)(false testimony by prosecution witness concerning consideration received is material); Lewis v. Commissioner, 790 F.3d 109 (2nd Cir. 2015)(evidence that State's key witness was coached by detective was exculpatory and impeaching). Improperly undisclosed information will be found to be material if there is a "reasonable probability that, had the evidence been disclosed to the defense, the result of the proceeding would have been different." (internal quotation marks omitted) United States v. Bagley, 473 U.S. 667, 682 (1985).

In determining whether undisclosed evidence was "material" in violation of Brady, the cumulative effect of all suppressed evidence favorable to the defendant is considered, rather than each item individually. Kyles v. Whitley, 514 U.S. at 440.

c. Perjured Testimony

The State's *knowing* proffer of perjured testimony is prohibited. It violates due process of law under both the state and federal constitutions. See Giglio v. United States, 405 U.S. 150 (1972)(due process bars prosecution from knowingly using material false testimony to obtain conviction and any conviction so obtained is invalid); Mooney v. Holohan, 294 U.S. 103 (1935)(prosecutor may not obtain conviction by presentation of testimony known by him to be perjured). Due process of law is equally violated when the State does not elicit the perjured testimony, but learns of its character and fails to correct it. See State v. Paradise, 213 Conn. 388, 399-400 (1990), overruled in part on other grounds, State v. Skakel, 276 Conn. 633, 693 (2006), cert. denied, 549 U.S. 1030 (2008).

Whether the State's *unknowing* proffer of perjured testimony is a violation of due process of law has not yet been decided by the Connecticut Supreme Court. Gould v. Commissioner, 301 Conn. 544, 569-71 and n.18 (2011). The Second Circuit, however, has taken the position that a due process violation results. See Ortega v. Duncan, 333 F.3d 102, 108 (2nd Cir. 2003)("[W]hen false testimony is provided by a government witness without the prosecutor's knowledge, due process is violated ... if the testimony was material and the court is left with a firm belief that but for the perjured testimony, the defendant would most likely not have been convicted."); Sanders v. Sullivan, 863 F.2d 218, 222-27 (2nd Cir. 1988) (perjured testimony can amount to a federal due process violation that warrants a new trial even if the state-court prosecutor did not know the testimony was perjured when presented), aff'd after remand, 900 F.2d 601, 602-07 (2nd Cir. 1990).

d. Newly Discovered Evidence

An attack on the judgment based on newly discovered evidence is permissible in habeas. See General Statutes § 52-470(e).

A claim of newly discovered evidence can, in certain instances, be brought in a petition for new trial pursuant to General Statutes §§ 54-95(a) and 52-270(a) and Practice Book § 42-55. This right, however, is limited by General Statutes § 52-582 which holds that "[n]o petition for a new trial in any civil or criminal proceeding shall be brought but within three years next after the rendition of the judgment or decree complained of, except that a petition based on DNA (deoxyribonucleic acid) evidence that was not discoverable or available at the time of the original trial may be brought at any time after the discovery or availability of such new evidence." A petition for new trial under General Statutes §§ 54-95(a) and 52-270(a) and Practice Book § 42-55 must be brought in the trial court. The test used in the trial court to decide the petition is "'whether an injustice was done and whether it is probable that on a new trial a different result would be reached.'" Summerville v. Warden, 229 Conn. 397, 425-26 (1994) (quoting Taborsky v. State, 142 Conn. 619, 623 (1955)); see also Asherman v. State, 202 Conn. 429, 434 (1987)(articulating four sub-parts of the test); Reilly v. State, 32 Conn. Sup. 349, 356 (Speziale, J.). The petitioner bears the burden of proof on a petition for new trial and the standard of proof is "preponderance of the evidence." Seebeck v. State, 246 Conn. 514, 545 (1998).

When the newly discovered evidence is a recantation of trial testimony by an original criminal trial witness, the test set forth in Pradlik v. State, 131 Conn. 682 (1945), determines whether the petition for new trial should be granted. See Johnson v. State, 36 Conn. App. 59, 64-65 (Pradlik applies to recantations), cert. denied, 231 Conn. 946 (1994). The test provides that a new trial should be granted when: "(a) The court is reasonably well satisfied that the testimony given by a material witness is false. (b) That without it the jury might have reached a different conclusion. (c) That the party seeking the new trial was taken by surprise when the false testimony was given and was unable to meet it or did not know of its falsity until after the trial." Pradlik v. State, 131 Conn. at 687 (quoting Larrison v. United States, 24 F.2d 82, 87 (7th Cir. 1928)); accord Johnson v. State, 36 Conn. App. at 65; see also Morant v. State, 68 Conn. App. 137, 150-160, cert. denied, 260 Conn. 914 (2002); Channer v. State, 54 Conn. App. 620, 627, cert. denied, 251 Conn. 910 (1999).

Habeas counsel must assess whether a newly discovered evidence claim can or should be brought in the trial court instead of the habeas court. The considerations will include the differing statute of limitations, see § 52-582 (statute of limitations for new trial petitions); § 52-470(c)(d)(e)(f)(statute of limitations for habeas petitions), and the differing standards of proof. See Summerville v. Warden, 229 Conn. at 424-33 (on new trial petition, preponderance of evidence standard, probability of different result); Miller v. Commissioner, 242 Conn. 745, 747, 791-92, 800 (1997)(on habeas petition, clear and convincing evidence standard, no reasonable fact finder would convict). Habeas counsel should also be mindful of the Connecticut Supreme Court's holding in Gould v. Commissioner, 301 Conn. 544 (2011), that a recantation does not constitute clear and convincing evidence of actual innocence, to the extent an actual innocence claim is alleged in the habeas petition. Id. at 546-65.

When a claim of newly discovered evidence is brought in a habeas petition, it should be pled as a freestanding claim. Whether it should also be couched in an ineffective assistance of counsel claim depends upon the facts and circumstances of the case.

e. Actual Innocence

An attack on the judgment based on a claim of actual innocence is permissible in habeas. See General Statutes § 52-470(f); see also Miller v. Commissioner, 242 Conn. 745, 747, 791-803 (1997)(delineating the standard that a habeas petitioner who claims actual innocence must meet in order to gain a new trial).

The imprisonment of a person for a crime he or she did not commit violates due process of law. See Jackson v. Commissioner, 227 Conn. 124, 132 n.7 (1993); Lozada v. Warden, 223 Conn. 834, 840 (1992). That recognition was reflected in Summerville v. Warden, 229 Conn. 397, 422 (1994), when the Connecticut Supreme Court held that "a substantial claim of actual innocence is cognizable by way of a petition for a writ of habeas corpus, even in the absence of proof by the petitioner of an antecedent constitutional violation that affected the result of his criminal trial." The Court observed that it would offend due process to ignore actual innocence claims in the name of upholding judgments or honoring the principle of finality. Id. When a substantial claim of actual innocence is brought in a habeas petition, the claim is known as a "freestanding" claim of actual innocence. Miller v. Commissioner, 242 Conn. at 788 n.28.

In Miller v. Commissioner, supra, 242 Conn. 745, the Connecticut Supreme Court determined the standard of proof necessary to sustain a claim of actual innocence brought in a habeas petition. Drawing from Herrera v. Collins, 506 U.S. 390 (1993) and In re Clark, 5 Cal. 4th 750, 766, 855 P.2d 729, 21 Cal. Rptr.2d 509 (1993), the Court held that a petitioner advancing a freestanding claim of actual innocence "must establish by clear and convincing evidence that, taking into account all the evidence - both the evidence adduced at the original criminal trial and the evidence adduced at the habeas corpus trial - he is actually innocent of the crime of which he stands convicted .... [and], that, after considering all of that evidence and the inferences drawn therefrom ..., no reasonable fact finder would find the petitioner guilty of the crime." 242 Conn. at 747; see Id. at 791-92, 794, 799-800; see also Clarke v. Commissioner, 249 Conn. 350, 355 (1999).

"'[F]actual' and 'actual' innocence have the same meaning and are used interchangeably...." Miller, 242 Conn. at 787 n.26. In Gould v. Commissioner, 301 Conn. 544 (2011), the Connecticut Supreme Court elaborated on the meaning of "actual innocence" under Miller. Id. at 546. The Court held that "[a]ctual innocence is not demonstrated merely by showing that there was insufficient evidence to prove guilt beyond a reasonable doubt. ... Rather, actual innocence is demonstrated by affirmative proof that the petitioner did not commit the crime. ... Affirmative proof of actual innocence is that which might tend to establish that the petitioner *could not* have committed the crime even though it is unknown who committed the crime, that a *third party* committed the crime or that *no* crime actually occurred. ... Clear and convincing proof of actual innocence does not, however, require the petitioner to establish that his or her guilt is a factual impossibility." (internal citations omitted; emphasis in original) Id. at 560-64; see also Jackson v. Commissioner, 149 Conn. App. 681, 705-07, cert. granted on other grounds, 313 Conn. 901 (2014).

The "[Connecticut] Supreme Court has deemed the issue of whether a habeas petitioner must support his claim of actual innocence with newly discovered evidence an open question in [Connecticut] habeas jurisprudence...." Jackson v. Commissioner, 149 Conn. App. at 707-08. The Connecticut Appellate Court, however, has concluded that the petitioner must "'demonstrate[] that the evidence put forth in support of [the] claim of actual innocence is newly discovered.... This evidentiary burden is satisfied if a petitioner can demonstrate, by a preponderance of the evidence, that the proffered evidence could not have been discovered prior to the petitioner's criminal trial by the exercise of due diligence.'" Jackson, 149 Conn. App. at 708 (quoting Gaston v. Commissioner, 125 Conn. App. 553, 558-59, cert. denied, 300 Conn. 908 (2011)); see generally Schlup v. Delo, 513 U.S. 298, 316 (1995)(newly discovered evidence used to support an actual innocence claim may include "exculpatory scientific evidence, trustworthy eyewitness accounts, or critical physical evidence").

In Gould v. Commissioner, supra, 301 Conn. 544, the Connecticut Supreme Court held that a credible recantation of testimony that was the sole evidence of guilt at trial does not constitute clear and convincing evidence of actual innocence, as required under Miller. Gould, 301 Conn. at 546-64. "[T]he Miller test ... requires affirmative evidence that the petitioner[] did not commit the crime[] of which [the petitioner] [was] convicted, not simply the discrediting of evidence on which the conviction rested." Id. at 546-47; see also Jackson v. Commissioner, 149 Conn. App. at 712-14.

f. Miller-Graham

In Graham v. Florida, 560 U.S. 48, 82 (2010), the Supreme Court held that life-without-parole sentences imposed on juveniles convicted of non-homicide offenses violate the Eighth Amendment's prohibition of cruel and unusual punishment and that such violation is corrected only by providing the defendant with a meaningful opportunity to obtain release from prison based on demonstrated personal reform. In Miller v. Alabama, 567 U.S. __, 132 S.Ct. 2455 (2012), the Supreme Court concluded that mandatory life-without-parole sentences for juveniles convicted of homicide offenses likewise violate the Eighth Amendment and such violation is remedied only by affording the defendant an individualized sentencing where his or her youthfulness as a mitigating factor is considered before the sentence is fixed.

In Montgomery v. Louisiana, 577 U.S. ___, No. 14-280 (Jan. 27, 2016), the Supreme Court held that Miller's prohibition on mandatory life-without-parole sentences for juvenile homicide offenders announced a new rule that, under the United States Constitution, is retroactive. Earlier, in Casiano v. Commissioner, 317 Conn. 52 (2015), the Connecticut Supreme Court concluded that Miller is retroactive. The Court further concluded that Miller embraces non-mandatory sentences that are the functional equivalent of a life sentence, including the fifty-year sentence under review in that case.

Going forward, trial counsel's failure at sentencing to argue a juvenile's character, background and history in mitigation of the punishment will constitute deficient performance under Strickland. As such, the habeas petition should allege counsel's missteps as a breach of both the federal and state constitutional guarantee of effective assistance of counsel and the federal and state constitutional guarantee to be free of cruel and unusual punishment.

With regard to the sentences imposed on juveniles before Miller-Graham, habeas counsel must consider whether the habeas court is the proper court in which to raise the claim initially or at all. It appears that the proper court to seek sentence relief under Miller-Graham, at least initially, is the trial court pursuant to Practice Book § 43-22 *Correction of Illegal Sentence.* See Cobham v. Commissioner, 258 Conn. 30, 38 (2001)("[B]efore seeking to correct an illegal sentence in the habeas court, a defendant either must raise the issue on direct appeal or file a motion pursuant to § 43-22 with the trial court."); see also State v. McNellis, 15 Conn. App. 416, 444 (discussing when a motion under § 43-22 is proper), cert. denied 209 Conn. 809 (1988). Seeking relief in the habeas court without first seeking relief in the trial court may expose the petition to the defense of procedural default and may subsequently give rise to an allegation of ineffective assistance of habeas counsel.

g. Jail Credit & Good Time Credit

i. Jail Credit

Jail credit, including pretrial confinement credit, is authorized under General Statutes §18-97, et seq. A claim that jail credit was erroneously withheld is permissible in habeas under General Statutes § 52-466. See Delevieleuse v. Manson, 184 Conn. 434, 439 (1981)(review through habeas petition the statutory right to appropriate jail credit). This is especially true if the credit was withheld because of ineffective assistance of counsel. See Gonzalez v. Commissioner, 308 Conn. 463 (2013)(Sixth Amendment and Article First, § 8 confer right to effective assistance of counsel in jail credit matters).

Cases that illuminate the application of jail credit are Payton v. Albert, 209 Conn. 23 (1988)(inmate cannot bank jail credit to reduce subsequent sentences); Wright v. Commissioner, 216 Conn. 220 (1990)(inmate, if resentenced, must get credit for time served for same offense); Harris v. Commissioner, 271 Conn. 808 (2004)(when jail credit is earned simultaneously in multiple files, the credit will be applied against the concurrent sentence that is imposed first); Cox v. Commissioner, 271 Conn. 844 (2004)(same); Hunter v. Commissioner, 271 Conn. 856 (2004)(same); and Washington v. Commissioner, 287 Conn. 792, 827 (2008)(Harris, Cox, and Hunter are retroactive and jail credit can be recalculated).

Before a jail credit claim is alleged in a habeas petition, habeas counsel should contact DOC records specialists Mary Jane Steele or Michelle DeVeau at 860-292-3471 to learn more about the computation of the petitioner's credit.

If habeas counsel's investigation establishes that jail credit has been denied due to an obvious misstep by defense counsel or an error in the trial court clerk's file, habeas counsel is well-served to contact the State's Attorney's Office. The State's Attorney's Office will often agree to a correction in the trial court record, so long as the denial of credit is through no fault of the defendant. The DOC, upon receipt of the corrected record, will make the necessary recalculation and apply the appropriate credit. Thus, contacting the State's Attorney's Office may eliminate the need to file an amended petition charging the denial of jail credit. If an amended petition is filed, however, the same equitable disposition can still be reached.

If habeas counsel's investigation reveals that jail credit has been denied due to the DOC's interpretation of a statute or court decision, a claim will have to be brought in the petition or amended petition. The State's Attorney's Office will almost never agree to relief. To the extent such a claim is brought, habeas counsel must secure copies of the trial court clerk's file and the transcripts of the relevant trial court proceedings for introduction at the habeas trial. Practice Book Section 23-36 provides for the filing of a copy of the clerk's file and the relevant transcripts in the habeas court. Likewise, habeas counsel must subpoena the client's DOC records that bear on jail credit. The testimony of a DOC official may also be necessary and, if so, should be obtained by subpoena.

Securing the foregoing items for introduction at the

habeas trial is also necessary if the basis of the claim is an error by defense counsel that for one reason or another, the State's Attorney's Office cannot agree to rectify.

ii. Good Time Credit

Good time credit is authorized under General Statutes § 18-7a. A claim that good time credit was erroneously withheld is permissible in habeas under General Statutes § 52-466. See Santiago v. Commissioner, 39 Conn. App. 674, 682-83 (1995)("loss of earned statutory good time credits ... sufficient to implicate a recognized liberty interest"); compare Abed v. Commissioner, 43 Conn. App. 176, 182 ("no liberty interest in unearned statutory good time credits"), cert. denied, 239 Conn. 937 (1996). Such a claim, however, will probably not derive from ineffective assistance of counsel because the deprivation will probably have occurred well after counsel's exit from the case. Thus, the claim will rest on due process of law. See Santiago v. Commissioner, 39 Conn. App. at 682 ("While there is no fourteenth amendment right for an inmate to receive[] good time credits, when a state creates a right to good time credits, it is 'required by the Due Process Clause to insure that the state-created right is not arbitrarily abridged.'" (quoting Wolff v. McDonnell, 418 U.S. 539, 557 (1994))). Article First, §§ 8 and 9 of the state constitution should also be cited in support of the claim.

Before a good time credit claim is alleged in a habeas petition, habeas counsel should contact DOC records specialists Mary Jane Steele or Michelle DeVeau at 860-292-3471 to learn more about the denial or forfeiture of the petitioner's credit.

h. Parole Eligibility

A claim that parole under General Statutes § 54-125a, et seq. was wrongly denied is not permissible in habeas. The habeas court has no jurisdiction to decide a claim concerning parole eligibility or the denial of parole. See Baker v. Commissioner, 281 Conn. 241 (2007)(habeas court lacks jurisdiction of claims concerning inmate classification and parole eligibility dates, as there is no liberty interest in parole eligibility); Vincenzo v. Warden, 26 Conn. App. 132, 142-43 (1991)(habeas court lacks jurisdiction because no liberty interest in release on parole); see also Johnson v. Commissioner, 258 Conn. 804 (2002)(85% law prospective only). Accordingly, a claim that the inmate was impermissibly denied parole should not be included in a habeas petition.

CHAPTER 19.

HABEAS DISCOVERY RULES

A. Petitioner's Discovery Request – Generally

It is appropriate and often necessary to serve a discovery request or motion on the respondent. Discovery is authorized in Practice Book § 23-38. The petitioner is permitted to obtain "[a] list of witnesses" under subsection (a)(1), "[a] statement of the subject matter upon which any expert is expected to testify" under subsection (a)(2), and "[a] statement of the opinions the expert is expected to render and the ground for each opinion" under subsection (a)(3). Subsection (b) permits "[t]he parties [to] cooperatively engage in informal discovery" and subsection (c), upon motion, authorizes the Court to "order such other limited discovery as the judicial authority determines will enhance the fair and summary disposal of the case." Such request or motion should also cite Practice Book § 40-9 (permitting defense experts to participate in testing), § 40-12 (permitting reasonable defense testing), and § 40-39 (compelling the prosecution to do comparison testing upon motion of the defense). Further, such request or motion should cite Bracy v. Gramley, 520 U.S. 899, 908-09 (1997)("[w]here specific allegations before the court show reason to believe that the petitioner may, if the facts are fully developed, be able to demonstrate that he is ... entitled to relief, it is the duty of the courts to provide the necessary facilities and procedures for an adequate inquiry")(internal quotation marks omitted; citation omitted); Giles v. Maryland, 386 U.S. 66, 74 (1967) (prosecution has a duty to disclose and/or make available any evidence that could be used in obtaining favorable evidence); and State v. Hammond, 221 Conn. 264, 292-93 (1992)(State has ethical duty, even after trial, to assist in pursuit of relevant, exculpatory evidence). The request or motion cannot be denied on the ground that the examination and testing might hamper a future prosecution if the writ of habeas corpus is granted. This is because there is no State interest that justifies the continued incarceration of a person who is actually or factually innocent. See Summerville v. Warden, 229 Conn. 397, 422 (1994). The very nature of the Great Writ of habeas corpus demands that an injustice be corrected not perpetuated.

Depositions are permitted in certain circumstances, but only with the permission of the habeas court. See Practice Book § 23-39.

B. Petitioner's Discovery Request – Example

The following is an example of a motion for forensic testing, specifically, mtDNA testing, in a habeas case. Due to the motion's age, all citations should be shepardized.

* * *

MOTION FOR DNA TESTING

Petitioner, pursuant to Practice Book Sections 23-38(c)("limited discovery [permissible if it] will enhance the fair and summary disposal of the case"), 40-9, 40-12 and 40-39, Bracy v. Gramley, 117 S.Ct. 1793, 1799 (1997)("[w]here specific allegations before the court [in a habeas case] show reason to believe that the petitioner may, if the facts are fully developed, be able to demonstrate that he is ... entitled to relief, it is the duty of the courts to provide the necessary facilities and procedures for an adequate inquiry")(internal quotation marks omitted; citation omitted), and State v. Hammond, 221 Conn. 264, 292-93 (1992)(State has ethical duty, even after trial, to assist in pursuit of relevant, exculpatory evidence), renews his motion for mitochondrial DNA (hereinafter "mtDNA") testing on certain hairs allegedly seized from the trunk of Petitioner's car, which evidence has been secured at Mitotyping Technologies, LLC, in State College, Pennsylvania since July, 2001, but which awaits further order of the habeas court before testing can commence.

REFUSAL TO PERMIT mtDNA TESTING ON THE HAIRS WOULD DENY PETITIONER THE OPPORTUNITY TO PRESENT EXCULPATORY EVIDENCE AND WOULD SIGNIFICANTLY IMPAIR PETITIONER'S ABILITY TO PREVAIL ON HIS PETITION, ALL CONTRARY TO A GROWING NATIONAL MOVEMENT TO ENSURE THAT WRONGFULLY CONVICTED PERSONS HAVE AN OPPORTUNITY TO ESTABLISH THEIR INNOCENCE THROUGH DNA TESTING.

A. The Claims

Paragraphs 12. k. iii and 13 of Count One of Petitioner's Second Amended Petition collectively allege that trial counsel rendered ineffective assistance under the state and federal constitutions when counsel failed to have scientific testing conducted on the hairs purportedly found by police in the trunk of Petitioner's car and on the victim's head hairs (which hairs were pulled at the autopsy), all for the purpose of demonstrating that such hairs are not "microscopically similar" and are not from the same source. (TT. 2/115; 3/13; 8/145-50; 9/11-12, 9/43; 10/43-47, 10/50-51, 10/60-61; 11/8-10; see also State's Exhibits 13 (autopsy hairs), 74 (hairs recovered from car trunk), 79 and 79a (photo boards of mounted hairs); State v. W*********, Conn. at __, __) Put another way, counsel erred in failing to have testing performed that would have demonstrated that the hairs allegedly found in the trunk of Petitioner's car are not those of the victim. Paragraphs 11 and 14-17 of Count Three of the Second Amemded Petition collectively allege that even if testing (or certain testing) was not reasonably available at the time of trial, such testing today could/will yield new exculpatory information that would support, in whole or in part, Petitioner's claim of actual and/or factual innocence. The failure of the habeas court to allow such testing would, of course, be fatal to both the factual claim, i.e., that the hairs found in the trunk of the car are not those of the victim, and the legal claims, i.e., that Petitioner has been prejudiced by counsel's failure and/or that he is actually innocent.

B. The Evidence And Its Significance

The hairs allegedly found in the trunk of Petitioner's car

were arguably the most significant piece of evidence at trial and were not cumulative to other evidence presented by the State. Dr. Lee testified that the hairs seized from the car trunk were "microscopically similar" to the head hairs pulled from the victim at the autopsy. (TT. 2/115; 3/13; 10/43-61; State v. W********, __ Conn. at __, __) Dr. Lee also testified that he observed reddish brown crust on the surface of the hairs and that subsequent presumptive testing reacted positive for the presence of blood.[1] (TT. 10/62-72; 11/7-8) While the State's case against Petitioner was circumstantial,[2] the hairs recovered from the trunk of the car were the only piece of evidence arguably belonging to and/or originating from the victim that was found in Petitioner's constructive possession. The hairs provided a direct physical link between Petitioner and the victim that

---

[1]The results of the presumptive blood test on the hairs should not have been admitted into evidence at trial. See State v. Moody, 214 Conn. 616, 627-30 (1990). The failure to object at trial on grounds of relevance and to raise this evidentiary error on appeal are two additional claims being raised by Petitioner in his Second Amended Petition. See Count One, Para. 12. e. iv; Count Two, Para. 12. a.

[2]See TT. 18/8-9 (State's Attorney Connelly's jury summation: "Now, this case, again right up front this is what we call a circumstantial case .... Circumstantial evidence, the evidence that we have in this case can't be changed because what is it? It's cloth, it's fiber, it's hair, it's metal rivets, it's metal bra hooks.").

was otherwise absent from the case. Consequently, the importance of the hairs cannot be downplayed by emphasizing the many other items of circumstantial evidence that comprised the State's case. The hairs allegedly recovered from the car trunk did not go unnoticed by the jury. During the trial, the jury sent a note inquiring where State's Exhibit 74 had come from. (TT. 10/75; 18/39-40) Later, the State focused on the hairs in its closing argument by reminding the jury that hairs similar to the known head hairs of the victim were found in the trunk of Petitioner's car and that the hairs had blood on them. (TT. 18/40 (State's Attorney Connelly: "Hair similar to [the victim's] was found in [the defendant's] car with blood on it."); see also 18/39-41, 18/169-70) The State also reminded the jury that next to the hairs in the trunk were the blue fiber or fibers that connected Petitioner and his car to the important fire site. (TT. 18/35-41, 18/169-70)

Mitochondrial DNA testing that demonstrates that the hairs allegedly recovered from the trunk of Petitioner's car are not those of the victim would obviously contradict the trial testimony and the reasonable inferences that were available to the jury to draw, and would thus support Petitioner's claim of actual innocence. See State v. Hammond, 221 Conn. at 268 ("One cogent reason for overturning the verdict of a jury is that the verdict is based on conclusions that are physically impossible.") The hairs were not cumulative to other evidence presented by the State, but rather represented the only piece of physical evidence linking Petitioner and the victim. There was no other evidence recovered from Petitioner's person, dwelling or car that belonged to or originated from the victim. In a universe of circumstantial evidence, the hairs represented the only item of the victim that was found in Petitioner's constructive possession. There was no other evidence that physically connected Petitioner and the victim. Because of their significance, the hairs were a key feature of the States closing argument. (TT. 18/39-41, 18/169-70) Consequently, exculpatory mtDNA results, coupled with a proper ruling on the admissibility of presumptive blood test results, see State v. Moody, 214 Conn. 616, 627-30 (1990), would cast the State's case in a fundamentally different light. Further, such exculpatory evidence, joined with Dr. Wecht's opinion that the evidence knife (State's Ex. 69) was not the knife or the type of knife used to cause the victim's death, would support Petitioner's claim of actual innocence. Still further, such evidence, joined with Dr. Wecht's testimony, would, notwithstanding the balance of the State's case, produce a different result on retrial. See Miller v. Commissioner, 242 Conn. 745, 747, 791-803 (1997)(delineating the standard that a habeas petitioner who claims actual innocence must meet in order to gain a new trial).

C. Mitochondrial DNA Testing

At trial in 1988, Dr. Lee testified that DNA testing might someday enable scientists to determine the origin of a particular hair. (TT. 3/12-15; 10/5-13, 10/43-47, 10/50-71; 11/7-13) That day came in 1996 when the Federal Bureau of Investigation became the first lab to conduct mitochondrial DNA testing, which is the only type of DNA testing that can discern a DNA pattern from hair shafts that contain no roots. (Nuclear DNA testing can only be performed on hairs that have roots attached.)

Mitochondrial DNA analysis is widely accepted in the scientific community as reliable. It has been subjected to peer review and countless scientific articles have been published about it. The FBI laboratory has validated the process and determined its rate of error. The only drawbacks to mitochondrial DNA testing for purposes of exclusion are that it is expensive, time-consuming, and requires a highly stable environment and special level of expertise to per-form. See A Comeback for Hair Evidence, 84 A.B.A.J. 66 (May, 1998).

Mitochondrial DNA testing is less discriminating than nuclear DNA testing because, since all individuals in a maternal lineage share the same mitochondrial DNA sequence, it is not a unique identifier. However, the statistical frequency of any given DNA sequence is only significant when there is a match. The discriminatory power of any DNA test, nuclear or mitochondrial, is irrelevant in the context of an exclusion. See State v. Hammond, 221 Conn. at 280 n. 8.

Many cases have been tried in the United States using mitochondrial DNA evidence and the method has been found reliable and admissible in several jurisdictions. See State v. Council, 515 S.E.2d 508 (S.C. 1999); State v. Underwood, 518 S.E.2d 231 (Ct.App.N.C. 1999); State v. Scott, 33 S.W.2d 759 (Tenn. 2000); People v. Klinger, 713 N.Y.S. 2d 823 (N.Y. 2000). Importantly, Connecticut recently joined those jurisdictions when our Supreme Court in State v. Pappas, 256 Conn. 854 (2001), approved the admissibility of mitochondrial DNA evidence. Id. at 866-90. The Connecticut Supreme Court found that the procedures used to extract and chart the chemical bases of mtDNA are scientifically valid and generally accepted in the scientific community. Id.

Accordingly, the habeas court can have no reservations about permitting mtDNA testing on the hairs. The testing would be performed by Mitotyping Technologies, LLC, an accredited lab which is devoted exclusively to the forensic applications of mtDNA analysis and which has often been requested by the Connecticut State Police Forensic Science

Lab to perform mtDNA testing on prosecution evidence.

D. Since The Parties Last Appeared Before The Habeas Court, The National Movement To Afford Wrongly Convicted Persons The Means To Establish Their Innocence Has Intensified

Because of the extensive press coverage of wrongful convictions and the phenomenon of DNA exonerations, the movement to afford wrongly convicted persons the means to establish their innocence has intensified during the last three years. Thirty states now have statutes addressing post-conviction DNA testing. (See Exhibit E: Innocence Project @ *www.innocenceproject.org*: Complete Legislation Listing, attached hereto.) All of these laws guarantee the availability of post-conviction DNA testing, where such testing may conclusively establish guilt or innocence or may have significant probative value to a finder of fact.

The federal government has also begun to enact measures that would ensure the availability of post-conviction DNA testing. The recently proposed Innocence Protection Act would grant any inmate convicted of a federal crime the right to petition a federal court for DNA testing, where such testing would support a claim of innocence. (See Exhibit F: Senate Bill 486, attached hereto.) The Act is a response to the emerging evidence of wrongful convictions, the power of DNA testing and the inability of convicted prisoners to obtain DNA testing. The Act has been endorsed by the Senate Judiciary Committee and is expected to be enacted by the House and Senate later this year. An additional feature of the Act is that it would withhold federal funds to any state that fails to make post-conviction DNA testing available.

Connecticut has also begun to consider measures that would ensure post-conviction DNA testing. Section 6 of Substitute Senate Bill No. 608, An Act Concerning The DNA Data Bank, provided that post-convicted persons could make application for DNA testing to support a claim of actual innocence. The Bill died in the Senate because of the high cost of funding the expanded data bank. (See Exhibit G: Substitute Senate Bill 608, attached hereto; see also Offender DNA Database Expansion Bills @ www.dnaresource.com, attached hereto.) It is anticipated that the legislation, including the post-conviction DNA testing provision, will be raised again (and eventually enacted). Three years ago, Connecticut passed Public Act 00-80, which amended General Statutes Section 52-582 by adding the exception authorizing a new trial petition based on DNA evidence not discoverable or available at the time of the original trial. Thus, it seems clear that Connecticut intends to follow the same path that the majority of states (and shortly the federal government) have taken on the issue of ensuring DNA testing to those who are wrongly convicted.

The movement to afford the wrongly convicted access to DNA testing has also been reflected in court decisions. For example, in Harvey v. Horan, No. 00-1123-A (E.D. Va. 2001), the United States District Court held that "the plaintiff ha[d] ... a due process right of access to the DNA evidence and to conduct DNA testing upon biological evidence, as such evidence could constitute material exculpatory material." Id. at 11 (See Exhibit H: 04/16/01 Memorandum Opinion, attached hereto.) Further, The District Court found that "denying the plaintiff access to potentially powerful exculpatory evidence would result in ... a miscarriage of justice." Id. at 12. In holding for the plaintiff, the Court specifically rejected the State of Virginia's argument, raised in its motion for summary judgment, as well as in an earlier motion to dismiss, that such testing should be denied per se because any favorable results obtained from the testing would not undermine the verdict. Id. at 6-13.

Likewise, in Charles v. Greenberg, 2000 WL 1838713 (E.D. La. 2000), the United States District Court held that there was a constitutional basis for access to biological evidence. See also infra pp. 20-23 (discussing the implications of Brady and due process on post-conviction

DNA testing requests).

Accordingly, an order permitting mtDNA testing to proceed on the hairs would not be inconsistent with recent court decisions or the major shifts in criminal justice legislation observed over the last three years.

THE REQUEST FOR mtDNA TESTING IS ALSO SUPPORTED ON CONSTITUTIONAL GROUNDS.

A. Incarcerating An Individual Pursuant To A Conviction For A Crime For Which He Is Innocent Violates The Due Process Clauses Of The United States and Connecticut Constitutions And The Prohibition Against Cruel And Unusual Punishment

The United States Supreme Court has recognized that incarcerating an individual for a crime he or she did not commit violates the Due Process Clause and the Eighth Amendment's prohibition against cruel and unusual punishment when a "truly persuasive" showing of actual innocence can be made.[3] See Herrera v. Collins, 506 U.S.

---

[3]Extending the principle of due process to include claims of actual innocence is also consistent with the Supreme Court's prior interpretation of the Due Process Clause. "[T]he full scope of the liberty guaranteed by the Due Process Clause cannot be found in or limited by the precise terms of the specific guarantees elsewhere provided in the Constitution. This `liberty' is not a series of isolated points .... It is a rational continuum which broadly speaking, includes freedom from all substantial arbitrary impositions and purposeless

390 (1993). The validity of a <u>Herrera</u> claim was recognized in <u>Schlup v. Delo</u>, 513 U.S. 298 (1995), where the Supreme Court held that a freestanding claim of actual innocence is cognizable if the federal habeas court is convinced that new facts unquestionably establish innocence. 513 U.S. at 317.

Although both <u>Herrera</u> and <u>Schlup</u> were cases in which the defendants faced the death penalty, the majority opinion in <u>Herrera</u> recognized that where a fundamental error results in an erroneous finding of guilt, "it would be rather strange jurisprudence ... which [holds] that under our Constitution [a defendant] could not be executed, but that he could spend the rest of his life in prison." <u>Herrera</u>, 506 U.S. at 405. Justice Blackmum, joined by Justices Stevens and Souter, also recognized in their dissenting opinion that it may violate the Eighth Amendment to

---

restraints ....'" <u>Planned Parenthood of Southeastern Pennsylvania v. Casey</u>, 505 U.S. 833, 848 (1992) (quoting <u>Poe v. Ulman</u>, 367 U.S. 497, 543 (1961)(Harlan, J., dissenting from dismissal on jurisdictional grounds)). Clearly, the conviction and imprisonment of an innocent person is the ultimate manifestation of "arbitrary impositions and purposeless restraints." "`In appropriate cases,' the principles of comity and finality that inform the concepts of cause and prejudice `must yield to the imperative of correcting a fundamentally unjust incarceration.'" <u>Schlup v. Delo</u>, 513 U.S. 298, 320 (1995)(quoting <u>Murray v. Carrier</u>, 477 U.S. 478, 495 (1986), quoting <u>Engle v. Isaac</u>, 456 U.S. 107, 135 (1982)).

imprison someone who is actually innocent. See Id. at 432 n.2. *A priori*, if the conviction of an innocent person is unconstitutional for purposes of execution, it must also be unconstitutional for purposes of imprisonment.

The Supreme Court has considered various standards of proof to sustain a claim of actual innocence, but has not adopted a particular one.[4]

The Connecticut Supreme Court has also recognized that incarcerating an individual for an offense he or she did not commit violates due process of law. See Jackson v. Commissioner, 227 Conn. 124, 132 n.7 (1993); Lozada v. Warden, 223 Conn. 834, 840 (1992); Bunkley v. Commissioner, 222 Conn. 444, 460-61 (1992). That

---

[4]Although *dicta* contained in the plurality opinion in Herrera enunciated several standards of proof, it is clear that the burden is a high one. Justice Rehnquist's majority opinion indicated that a "truly persuasive demonstration of actual innocence made after trial could render the execution of a defendant unconstitutional ...." 506 U.S. at 417. Justice O'Connor's concurring opinion (joined by Justice Kennedy) and Justice Blackmum's concurring opinion (joined by Justices Stevens and Souter) found that a "truly persuasive showing of `actual innocence'" would render the execu-tion of a defendant unconstitutional. Id., at 430. Justice White, also concurring, concluded that relief should be granted in cases where "no rational trier of fact could [find] proof of guilt beyond a reasonable doubt." Id., at 429; see Miller v. Commissioner, 242 Conn. at 745 (discussing the various standards of proof articulated in Herrera). In Schlup, the Court posited a standard where the facts "unquestionably establish" innocence. 513 U.S. at 317.

recognition was further reflected in <u>Summerville v. Warden</u>, 229 Conn. 397, 422 (1994), when the Court held that "a substantial claim of actual innocence is cognizable by way of a petition for a writ of habeas corpus, even in the absence of proof by the petitioner of an antecedent constitutional violation that affected the result of his criminal trial." The Court observed that it would offend due process to ignore actual innocence claims in the name of upholding judgments or honoring the principle of finality. <u>Id.</u>

Unlike the United States Supreme Court, the Connecticut Supreme Court has determined the standard of proof necessary to sustain a claim of actual innocence. Drawing from <u>Herrera</u> and <u>In re Clark</u>, 5 Cal. 4th 750, 766, 855 P.2d 729, 21 Cal. Rptr.2d 509 (1993), the Supreme Court in <u>Miller v. Commissioner</u>, <u>supra</u>, concluded that a petitioner advancing a freestanding claim of actual innocence "must establish by clear and convincing evidence that, taking into account all the evidence - both the evidence adduced at the original criminal trial and the evidence adduced at the habeas corpus trial - he is actually innocent of the crime of which he stands convicted .... [and], that, after considering all of that evidence and the inferences drawn therefrom ..., no reasonable fact finder would find the petitioner guilty of the crime." 242 Conn. at

747; see Id. at 791-92, 794, 799-800; see also Clarke v. Commissioner, 249 Conn. 350, 355 (1999).

Accordingly, due process continues to protect the innocent and wrongly convicted.

B. DNA Testing Can Establish Actual Innocence

DNA testing is precisely the type of "truly persuasive" evidence that can meet the "extraordinarily high" standard contemplated by the United States Supreme Court and the Connecticut Supreme Court when addressing actual innocence claims.[5] Unlike post-conviction confessions or recantations which historically have been distrusted, see Johnson v. State, 36 Conn. App. 59, 69 (1994)("Recantation as grounds for a new trial has always been viewed with skepticism."), exculpatory DNA results are objective, precise and absolutely reliable. Cf. State v. Hammond, 221 Conn. at 279-89 (Supreme Court concluding that it was undisputed, based on uncontroverted blood typing and DNA evidence, that it was scientifically impossible for the accused to have committed the sexual assault).

While the significance of an inclusion or "match"

---

[5]"DNA analysis promises to be the most important tool for human identification since Francis Galton developed the use of fingerprints for that purpose." The Evaluation of Forensic DNA Testing, Report of the National Research Council (1996) at v.

produced by DNA testing has been the subject of dispute in courts of several jurisdictions, evidence of a DNA exclusion has never been the subject of serious scientific or legal controversy. See State v. Hammond, 221 Conn. at 280 n. 8. As discussed above, mtDNA testing that demonstrates that the hairs allegedly recovered by police from Petitioner's car trunk are not those of the victim would contradict the trial evidence and the reasonable inferences drawn therefrom and would thus support Petitioner's claim of actual innocence. See State v. Hammond, 221 Conn. at 268 ("One cogent reason for overturning the verdict of a jury is that the verdict is based on conclusions that are physically impossible.") The hairs were not cumulative to other trial evidence, but rather represented the only piece of physical evidence directly connecting Petitioner to the victim. There was no other evidence found in Petitioner's constructive possession that belonged to or derived from the victim. Because of their importance, the hairs were prominently featured in the State's summation. (TT. 18/40 (State's Attorney Connelly: "Hair similar to [the victim's] was found in [the defendant's] car with blood on it."); see also 18/39-41, 18/169-70) Consequently, exculpatory mtDNA results, coupled with a proper ruling on the admissibility of presumptive blood test results, see State v. Moody, 214 Conn. at 627-30, would significantly weaken the State's case. Further, such exculpatory evidence, coupled with Dr. Wecht's opinion that the evidence knife (State's Ex. 69) was not the knife or the type of knife used to cause the victim's death, would support Petitioner's actual innocence claim and would alter the outcome of the trial. Accordingly, the significance of the hairs to the State's case and to Petitioner's claim of actual innocence cannot be minimized, so as to preclude mtDNA analysis.

C. Due Process Requires the State to Provide Petitioner With Any Exculpatory Evidence Which Is Material To Guilt Or Innocence

Connecticut courts have recognized that the Connecticut and federal due process provisions have similar meanings. State v. Linares, 32 Conn. App. 656, 661 n.9 (1993), aff'd in part, rev'd in part on other grounds, 232 Conn. 345 (1995). Under the Due Process Clause of the United States Constitution, the State must provide the petitioner with any exculpatory evidence in its possession which is material to guilt or innocence. See U.S. const. amends. V and XIV; see also Brady v. Maryland, 373 U.S. 83 (1963). This right includes the opportunity to introduce evidence and to have judicial findings based upon that evidence. Id.

The discovery rule in Brady evolves from the

fundamental right to a fair trial provided by the Fifth and Fourteenth Amendments to the United States Constitution. Brady, 373 U.S. at 86; see United States v. Agurs, 427 U.S. 97, 107 (1976); see also Pennsylvania v. Ritchie, 480 U.S. 39, 56 (1987); United States v. Bagley, 473 U.S. 667, 675 (1985). The concept of a fair trial imposes a constitutional duty on the prosecution to disclose evidence material to a defendant's guilt or innocence. Bagley, 473 U.S. at 674, 675; Brady, 373 U.S. at 87. The purpose of requiring disclosure is "not to displace the adversary system as the primary means by which truth is uncovered, but to ensure that a miscarriage of justice does not occur." Bagley, 473 U.S. at 765.

The quest for truth does not terminate with a defendant's conviction. As evidenced by the Connecticut Supreme Court's orders in Hammond, justice is served by permitting one who has been convicted of a crime to prove factual innocence, even if that undermines the finality of the conviction. The State remains bound by the constitutional rules of simple fairness that Brady and its progeny have established.

In addition, courts in other jurisdictions have concluded that the State is required, pursuant to Brady, to preserve and produce evidence for post-conviction examination. In Matter of Dabbs v. Vergari, 149 Misc.2d 844 (N.Y.Sup.Ct.

Westchester 1990), the court examined a defendant's right to post-conviction DNA testing in light of Brady and held that a defendant has a constitutional right, retained even after conviction, to be informed of exculpatory information in the State's possession. Id. at 848.

The due process analysis articulated in Dabbs has been adopted by courts in other jurisdictions which have ordered post-conviction DNA testing. See Sewell v. State, 592 N.E.2d 705, 708 (Ind.Ct.App. 1992)(fundamental fairness requires post-conviction discovery of rape kit and laboratory records notwithstanding a lack of strict compliance with normal statutory discovery procedures); State v. Thomas, 586 A.2d 250, 253 (N.J.Super.Ct.App.Div. 1991)(Constitution guarantees post-conviction discovery of rape kit in the prosecutor's possession which may yield material susceptible to DNA testing); Commonwealth v. Brison, 618 A.2d 420 (Pa.Super. 1992)(principles of justice require post-conviction discovery of samples taken from rape victim for purposes of DNA testing; testing ordered, defendant excluded, conviction vacated); Mebane v. State, 902 P.2d 494 (Ka.App. 1995)(fundamental fairness requires defendant be able to obtain DNA testing); Deberry v. State, 457 A.2d 744 (Del. 1983)(State required by *Brady* to preserve and produce defendant's clothing for post-conviction examination). These courts put aside procedural objections to post-conviction DNA testing, recognizing that it is unfair to deny an incarcerated person this powerful tool for establishing innocence:

> *Our system fails every time an innocent person is convicted no matter how meticulously the procedural requirements governing criminal trials are followed. That failure is even more tragic when an innocent person is sentenced to a prison term ....*

> *There is a possibility, if not a probability, that DNA testing now can put to rest the question of defendant's guilt ... We would rather permit the testing than sit by while a possibly innocent man ... languishes in prison ... [W]e will not elevate form so highly over substance that funda-mental justice is sacrified.*

State v. Thomas, 245 N.J.Super. at 435-36; see Sewell v. State, 592 N.E.2d at 708.

The federal courts, ruling on federal habeas petitions, have granted access to evidence and DNA testing where there is a likelihood that the test results could exonerate the defendant. See Jones v. Wood, 114 F.3d 1002 (9th Cir. 1997); Toney v. Gammon, 79 F.2d 693 (8th Cir. 1996).

Finally, it should be emphasized that the United States Supreme Court's rulings with respect to a duty to preserve potentially exculpatory evidence, a variant of the Brady obligation, also support granting Petitioner a right of access to the evidence. The leading case, <u>Arizona v. Youngblood</u>, 488 U.S. 51 (1988), concerned the destruction of rectal swabs containing semen which Youngblood claimed could prove his innocence through serological testing. Without proof that the swabs were destroyed in bad faith, the <u>Youngblood</u> court held that there was no constitutional violation. Nonetheless, there was never any dispute that Youngblood had a constitutional right to conduct serological testing on the swabs if they had been preserved because the swabs were potentially exculpatory evidence. 488 U.S. at 58.

Accordingly, due process requires that the Court permit Petitioner to go forward with mtDNA testing on the hairs.

<u>Conclusion</u>

The Great Writ of habeas corpus demands that an injustice be corrected not perpetuated. Denial of mtDNA testing to a person attempting to prove his innocence and wrongful conviction cannot be sustained on the ground that courts must ensure the finality of judgments or the preservation (of never to be used again) evidence. Simply stated, there is no principle of law or government interest that justifies the continued incarceration of an innocent person. See Summerville v. Warden, 229 Conn. at 422.

WHEREFORE, Petitioner requests that this Motion be granted.

* * *

C. Respondent's Discovery Request

A (reciprocal) discovery request or motion by the respondent pursuant to Practice Book § 23-38 is not uncommon. In IAC cases, habeas counsel should anticipate that the respondent will seek from the petitioner a copy of trial counsel's file and/or appellate counsel's file. Habeas counsel should also anticipate that the respondent will seek items or information that the petitioner intends to introduce in evidence at the habeas trial.

The respondent's request or motion must be reviewed to ensure that it is not beyond the scope of Practice Book § 23-38 or the claims plead in the amended petition. An objection must be filed to any request or motion that is overbroad, for information that is beyond the scope of § 23-38 or the claims plead in the petition remains confidential under the attorney-client privilege and/or Rule 1.6 of the Rules of Professional Conduct. This is so because an IAC claim pierces the attorney-client privilege and/or rule of confidentiality, see Breton v. Commissioner, 49 Conn. Supp. 592, 598-99 (Super. Ct. 2006)("[T]he petitioner does place the advice of his attorneys into question before this habeas court. In so doing, he impliedly waived his attorney-client privilege such that his lawyers are free to testify and speak with counsel for the respondent without invoking the former client's attorney-client privilege."); accord Hardison v. Commissioner, 152 Conn. App. 410, 421 (2014)("We conclude that the petitioner has waived the attorney-client privilege because the issues raised in his petition cannot be determined without examining [trial counsel's] advice, and, therefore, the habeas court did not err in denying the motion in limine to preclude her testimony"), but only with respect to what is alleged. Information or parts of trial counsel's file or appellate counsel's file that is unrelated to the claim plead is not relevant to the habeas litigation and, thus, is entitled to continued protection under the attorney-client privilege and/or the confidentiality rule. See Breton v. Commissioner, 49 Conn. Supp. at 600-01; see also Giordano v. United States, No. 3:11-cv-09 (MRK), 2011 U.S. Dist. LEXIS 27910, at *7 (D. Conn. Mar. 17, 2011)(when petitioner alleges IAC, the implied waiver of the attorney-client privilege "does not extend beyond what is needed to litigate the claim")(quoting Bittaker [v. Woodford], 331 F.3d 715, 722 (9th Cir. 2003)(en banc); accord United States v. Pinson, 584 F.3d 972, 978 (10th Cir. 2009)("[T]he court must impose a waiver no broader than needed to ensure the fairness of the proceedings before it." (internal quotation marks omitted)).

Additionally, if any information required to be disclosed pursuant to the respondent's request would impair the petitioner's rights at a retrial, habeas counsel should move for a protective order, citing Practice Book § 40-40, et seq. and the following authorities: United States v. Nicholson, 611 F.3d 191, 217 (4th Cir. 2010)(holding that petitioner was "entitled to a protective order prohibiting the Government from using privileged information revealed by [defense counsel] in litigating [petitioner's] actual conflict of interest claim"); Bittaker v. Woodford, 331 F.3d at 722-24 (affirming entry of protective order limiting implied waiver to habeas proceeding); Longo v. Premo, 326 P.3d 1152, 1161 (Ore. 2014)(holding that habeas petitioner was entitled to a protective order prohibiting use of trial counsel's information in subsequent proceedings); Commonwealth v. Chmiel, 738 A.2d 406, 424 (Pa. 1999)("Just as an attorney may not respond to allegations of ineffectiveness by disclosing client confidences unrelated to such allegations, so the client confidences properly disclosed by an attorney at an ineffectiveness hearing may not be imported into the client's subsequent trial on criminal charges.").

CHAPTER 20.

RESPONDENT'S DEFENSES

In its return to the amended petition, see Practice Book §§ 23-30 and 23-35(b), the respondent may raise one or more defenses and seek the dismissal of the petition. With the exception of the defense of successive petition, the habeas court must hold an evidentiary hearing before the motion is granted. See Mercer v. Commissioner, 230 Conn. 88, 93 (1994)("absent an explicit exception, an evidentiary hearing is always required before a habeas petition may be dismissed"); see also Carter v. Commissioner, 109 Conn. App. 300, 305-06 (2008)(evidentiary hearing always required unless previous petition and current petition allege the same grounds and current petition fails to state new facts or evidence not reasonably available at prior hearing).

The following are some of the common defenses:

A. Jurisdiction

The respondent, in its return, may contend that the habeas court lacks subject matter jurisdiction and that the habeas petition should be dismissed pursuant to Practice Book §§ 23-24(a)(1)(2)(3), 23-29(1), 23-30(b), 23-34 and/or 23-37. This is generally seen when the aim of the petition is something other than illegal confinement or the infringement of a constitutional right.

"A court has subject matter jurisdiction if it has the authority to hear a particular type of legal controversy.... Subject matter jurisdiction for adjudicating habeas petitions is conferred on the [habeas court] by General Statutes § 52-466, which gives it the authority to hear those petitions that allege illegal confinement or deprivation of liberty." (citation omitted) Abed v. Commissioner, 43 Conn. App. 176, 179, cert. denied, 239 Conn. 937 (1996); see Santiago v. Commissioner, 39 Conn. App. 674, 679 (1995) ("The scope of relief available through a petition for habeas corpus is limited. In order to invoke the trial court's subject matter jurisdiction in a habeas action, a petitioner must allege that he is illegally confined or has been deprived of his liberty."); see, e.g. Baker v. Commissioner, 281 Conn. 241 (2007)(habeas court lacks jurisdiction of claims concerning inmate classification and parole eligibility dates, as there is no liberty interest in parole eligibility); Vincenzo v. Warden, 26 Conn. App. 132, 142-43 (1991) (habeas court lacks jurisdiction because no liberty interest in release on parole).

In reply, see Practice Book §§ 23-31 and 29-35(c), habeas counsel should deny the allegation if counsel believes that subject matter jurisdiction exists. However, if habeas counsel believes there is merit to the defense, counsel should move to amend the pleading, citing Practice Book §§ 23-32 and 23-33, so as to allege the deprivation of a legally recognized constitutional right. In Reeves v. Commissioner, 119 Conn. App. 852, cert. denied, 296 Conn. 906 (2010), the Connecticut Appellate Court stated: "While our courts have been liberal in permitting amendments ... this liberality has limitations. Amendments should be made seasonably. Factors to be considered in passing on a motion to amend are the length of delay, fairness to the opposing parties and the negligence, if any, of the party offering the amendment." (internal quotation marks omitted; citation omitted) Id. at 864-65. These factors should be addressed in the motion.

B. Statute of Limitations

The statute of limitations for a habeas petition is set forth in General Statutes § 52-470(c)(d)(e)(f). If a claim in the petition appears to be time-barred, the respondent, in its return, may seek dismissal of the claim pursuant to Practice Book §§ 23-24(a)(1), 23-29(1)(5), 23-30(b), 23-34 and/or 23-37. In reply, see Practice Book §§ 23-31 and 23-35(c), habeas counsel should deny the allegation if good cause exists for the late filing, see General Statutes § 52-470(c)(d)(e); if the filing occurred before October 1, 2012, the effective date of the statute of limitations provision see General Statutes § 52-470; or if the statute of limitations does not apply because the claim concerns a death sentence, actual innocence or a condition of confinement. See General Statutes § 52-470(f). Habeas counsel should also explore, and if appropriate plead, any lack of advice that petitioner received from prior counsel on the statute of limitations.

C. Mootness

The respondent, in its return, may assert that the claims in the habeas petition are moot because the habeas court can no longer grant practical relief to the petitioner. As a result, the petition should be dismissed pursuant to Practice Book §§ 23-22(1), 23-24(a)(1)(3), 23-29(1)(4)(5), 23-

30(b), 23-34 and/or 23-37.

"Mootness ... implicates subject matter jurisdiction, which imposes a duty on the [trial] court to dismiss a case if the court can no longer grant practical relief to the parties.... Mootness presents a circumstance wherein the issue before the court has been resolved or had lost its significance because of a change in the condition of affairs between the parties.... A case becomes moot when due to intervening circumstances a controversy between the parties no longer exists." (internal quotation marks omitted; citation omitted) Paulino v. Commissioner, 155 Conn. App. 154, 160, cert. denied, 317 Conn. 912 (2015). "A case is considered moot if [the trial] court cannot grant the appellant any practical relief through its disposition of the merits...." (internal quotation marks omitted; citation omitted) Id. at 161.

A claim of mootness is overcome by demonstrating "(1) that there [is] an actual controversy between or among the parties to the dispute ... (2) that the interests of the parties [are] adverse ... (3) that the matter in controversy [is] capable of being adjudicated by judicial power ... and (4) that the determination of the controversy will result in practical relief to the complainant...." Id. With this framework in mind, if the respondent contends that the claims in the habeas petition are moot because the petitioner is not illegally confined, habeas counsel, in the reply, see Practice Book §§ 23-31 and 23-35(c), should deny the allegation if the petitioner was incarcerated or under the restraint of the judgment at the time the petition was filed. See supra A. *HABEAS CORUS JURISPRUDENCE* 2. *Custody.*

If the respondent contends that the habeas claims are moot because the petitioner has been deported, see Paulino v. Commissioner, supra, 155 Conn. App. 154, and Quiroga v. Commissioner, 149 Conn. App. 168, 170-74, cert. denied, 311 Conn. 950 (2014) for a discussion on the implications of deportation. Generally speaking, for the petition to continue to present an actual controversy, there must be some remaining collateral consequence of the judgment under attack that can be redressed by the litigation, such as the petitioner's ability to reenter the United States, see Perez v. Greiner, 296 F.3d 123, 126 (2nd Cir. 2002), or reenter without restrictions on his or her liberty. See United States v. Rivas-Gonzalez, 384 F.3d 1034, 1042 (9th Cir. 2004); United States v. Lares-Meraz, 452 F.3d 352, 354-56 (5th Cir. 2006). See supra A. *HABEAS CORUS JURISPRUDENCE 2. Custody.*

If the respondent contends that the habeas claims are moot because they have already been decided, see infra T. *RESPONDENT'S DEFENSES* 5. *Res Judicata & Collateral*

Estoppel.

D. Insufficiency

The respondent, in its return, may contend that a claim in the amended petition is insufficient or fails to state a cause of action and, accordingly, should be dismissed under Practice Book §§ 23-22(1), 23-24(a)(2)(3), 23-29(2)(5), 23-30(b), 23-34 and/or 23-37. See, e.g. Abed v. Commissioner, 43 Conn. App. 176, 182 ("Because the petitioner has no liberty interest in unearned statutory good time credits, he has failed to raise a legally cognizable claim upon which relief can be granted."), cert. denied, 239 Conn. 937 (1996). In reply, see Practice Book §§ 23-31and 29-35(c), habeas counsel should deny the allegation if counsel believes the claim provides sufficient notice or states a cause of action. See supra R. *AMENDED PETITION 2. Claims Inside & Outside the Record*. However, if habeas counsel believes there is merit to the defense, counsel should move to amend the pleading, citing Practice Book §§ 23-32 and 23-33 and addressing the factors set forth in Reeves v. Commissioner, 119 Conn. App. at 864-65.

E. Res Judicata & Collateral Estoppel

The respondent, in its return, may contend that a claim

or issue in the amended petition has already been decided and that the principle of res judicata (claim preclusion) or the principle of collateral estoppel (issue preclusion) bars re-litigation of the claim or issue. Thus, the claim or issue is subject to dismissal under Practice Book §§ 23-22(3), 23-29(3)(4)(5), 23-30(b), 23-34 and/or 23-37. "The related doctrines of res judicata and collateral estoppels are based on the public policy that a party should not be able to relitigate a matter that it already has had a fair and full opportunity to litigate." In re Ross, 272 Conn. 653, 661 (2005).

a. Res Judicata

The res judicata principle holds that

a former judgment on a claim, if rendered on the merits, is an absolute bar to a subsequent action [between the same parties] on the same claim.... To determine whether two claims are the same for purposes of res judicata, we compare the pleadings and judgment in the first action with the complaint in the subsequent action.... The judicial doctrine of res judicata is based on the public policy that a party should not be able to relitigate a matter which it already has had an opportunity to litigate.... [W]here a party has fully and fairly litigated his claims, he may be barred from future actions on matters not raised in the prior proceeding.

(internal quotation marks omitted; citations omitted) Thorpe v. Commissioner, 73 Conn. App. 773, 777 (2002); see also Bridges v. Commissioner, 97 Conn. App. 119, 122 ("The rule of claim preclusion prevents reassertion of the same claim regardless of what additional or different evidence or legal theories might be advanced in support of it." (internal quotation marks omitted; citation omitted)), cert. denied, 280 Conn. 921 (2006); see generally McCarthy v. Warden, 213 Conn. 289 (1989). The life or liberty interests at stake in habeas proceedings counsel against extending the res judicata principle to claims that could have been raised in earlier proceedings. See Johnson v. Commissioner, 288 Conn. 53, 67 (2008)("[I]n the habeas context, in the interest of ensuring 'that no one is deprived of liberty in violation of his or her constitutional rights ... the application of the doctrine of res judicata ... [is limited] to claims that actually have been raised and litigated in an earlier proceeding.'" (citation omitted)), overruled in part on other grounds, State v. Elson, 311 Conn. 726 (2014); see also Thorpe v. Commissioner, 73 Conn. App. at 778 n.7 ("Although the doctrine of res judicata in its fullest sense bars claims that *could have been raised* in a prior proceeding, such an application in the habeas corpus context would be unduly harsh.").

Hence, when the respondent raises res judicata as a defense, habeas counsel must review the trial record and appellate record to determine the precise nature of any previous claim and decision. See, e.g. Jefferson v. Commissioner, 99 Conn. App. 321, 323-26 (habeas claim that special parole sentence was illegal barred by res judicata because petitioner litigated the claim in the trial court on a motion to correct an illegal sentence), cert. denied, 281 Conn. 928 (2007); Bridges v. Commissioner, 97 Conn. App. at 121 (habeas claim that petitioner suffered ineffective assistance of counsel on Alford plea barred by res judicata because petitioner moved to withdraw the plea in the trial court on the ground of ineffective assistance of counsel); Thorpe, 73 Conn. App. at 778 (habeas claim that introduction of rifle in evidence at criminal trial violated the constitution not barred by res judicata because on direct appeal petitioner contended the introduction violated the rules of evidence). If, after such review, it is determined that the claims are not identical, habeas counsel should reply by denying the allegation and explaining the difference in the claims. See Practice Book §§ 23-31 and 29-35(c).

Also, while the Connecticut Supreme Court has held that the principle of res judicata applies to habeas proceedings, see In re Ross, 272 Conn. at 669, the Court has also explained that the principle's application should be tempered when a constitutional violation is asserted and life or liberty is at stake. See In re Ross, 272 Conn. at 662; see also James L. v. Commissioner, 245 Conn. 132, 142 n.11 (1998)("[T]he doctrines of res judicata and collateral estoppel ... are ordinarily inapplicable in the habeas corpus context. Conventional notions of finality of litigation have no place where life or liberty is at stake and the infringement of constitutional rights is alleged.... The inapplicability of res judicata, then, is inherent in the very role and function of the writ." (internal quotation marks omitted; citation omitted)); Thorpe, 73 Conn. App. at 779 n.7. Thus, in the reply, counsel should also assert the general inapplicability of the defense in habeas proceedings.

b. Collateral Estoppel

The collateral estoppel principle holds that

when an issue of ultimate fact has once been determined by a valid and final judgment, that issue cannot again be litigated between the same parties in any future lawsuit.... [Thus] [i]ssue preclusion arises when an issue is actually litigated and determined by a valid and final judgment, and that determination is essential to the judgment.

(internal quotation marks omitted; citation omitted) In re Ross, 272 Conn. at 661. " "'[T]he decision whether to apply the doctrine of collateral estoppels in any particular case should be made based upon a consideration of the doctrine's underlying policies.... These [underlying] purposes are generally identified as being (1) to promote judicial economy by minimizing repetitive litigation; (2) to prevent inconsistent judgments which undermine the integrity of the judicial system; and (3) to provide repose by preventing a person from being harassed by vexatious litigation.... Stability in judgments grants to parties and others the certainty in the management of their affairs which results when a controversy is finally laid to rest.'" In re Ross, 272 Conn. at 662 (quoting Cumberland Farms, Inc. v. Groton, 262 Conn. 45, 59 (2002)).

Accordingly, when the respondent raises collateral estoppel as a defense, habeas counsel must review the trial record and appellate record to determine the precise nature of any previous issue and ruling. If such review reveals that the issues are not identical, habeas counsel should reply by denying the allegation and explaining the distinction between the issues. See Practice Book §§ 23-31 and 29-35(c). Counsel, in the reply, should also assert the general inapplicability of the defense in habeas proceedings.

F. Procedural Default

The respondent, in its return, may assert that a claim in the amended petition is procedurally defaulted because it was not raised at trial or on appeal. Thus, it is subject to dismissal under Practice Book §§ 23-22(3), 23-29(5), 23-30(b), 23-34 and/or 23-37. This is sometimes seen when a fundamental right violation is raised for the first time in a habeas petition.

The defense of procedural default is an affirmative defense. If the respondent does not raise the defense of procedural default in its return, see Practice Book § 23-30(b), the defense is waived. Day v. Commissioner, 151 Conn. App. 754, cert. denied, 314 Conn. 936 (2014); Quint v. Commissioner, 99 Conn. App. 395, 403 (2007). If, however, the defense is raised in the return, habeas counsel must answer it in the reply, unless the amended petition itself puts the defense in dispute or otherwise asserts cause and prejudice. See Practice Book § 23-31(a)(c).

"The appropriate standard for reviewability of habeas claims that were not properly raised at trial ... or on direct appeal ... because of a procedural default is the cause and prejudice standard. Under this standard, the petitioner must demonstrate good cause for his failure to raise a claim at trial or on direct appeal and actual prejudice resulting from the impropriety claimed in the petition.... [T]he cause and prejudice test is designed to prevent full review of issues in habeas corpus proceedings that counsel did not raise at trial or on appeal for reasons of tactics, inadvertence or ignorance...." (internal quotation marks omitted; citation omitted) Cobham v. Commissioner, 258 Conn. 30, 40 (2001). Use of the cause and prejudice test in habeas proceedings began in Wainwright v. Sykes, 433 U.S. 72, 87 (1977). Connecticut utilizes the cause and prejudice test. See Johnson v. Commissioner, 218 Conn. 403, 419 (1991)(cause and prejudice test applied in habeas proceedings when respondent charges procedural default for failure to raise constitutional violation at trial); Jackson v. Commissioner, 227 Conn. 124 (1993)(cause and prejudice test applied in habeas proceedings when respondent charges procedural default for failure to raise constitutional violation on appeal).

The leading United States Supreme Court cases on procedural default are Wainwright v. Sykes, supra 433 U.S. 72; Engle v. Isaac, 456 U.S. 107 (1982); Reed v. Ross, 468

U.S. 1 (1984); Murray v. Carrier, 477 U.S. 478 (1986); and Coleman v. Thompson, 501 U.S. 722 (1991). These cases, and our own cases, collectively reveal what does and does not constitute "cause" for a procedural default. The following circumstances have been held to constitute "cause" for a procedural default— The failure of counsel to raise a claim for which there was no reasonable basis in existing law constitutes cause for a procedural default. See Murray v. Carrier, 477 U.S. at 488; Reed v. Ross, 468 U.S. at 15-16; Engle v. Isaac, 456 U.S. at 131. The failure of counsel to raise a claim because of "interference by officials," Brown v. Allen, 344 U.S. 443, 486 (1953), constitutes cause for a procedural default. See Murray, 477 U.S. at 488. An error by counsel that amounts to ineffective assistance of counsel constitutes cause for a procedural default. See Murray, 477 U.S. at 488, 496; Coleman v. Thompson, 501 U.S. at 754-56; cf. State v. Leecan, 198 Conn. 517, 541-42 (claim of ineffective assistance of counsel raised for first time in habeas petition does not violate deliberate bypass rule), cert. denied, 476 U.S. 1184 (1986); Valeriano v. Bronson, 209 Conn. 75, 85 (1988) (ineffective assistance of counsel claim for failing to raise claim on direct appeal automatically satisfies the deliberate bypass requirement). Overall, any "objective factor external to the defense [that] impeded counsel's efforts to comply with the State's procedural rule" constitutes cause for a procedural default. See Murray, 477 U.S. at 488.

The following circumstances have been held not to constitute "cause" for a procedural default— Absent exceptional circumstances, the strategic decisions of competent counsel do not constitute cause for a procedural default. See Wainwright, 433 U.S. at 91 n.14; Reed, 468 U.S. at 13-14. The failure of competent counsel to recognize a claim, or to raise a claim that he or she recognized, does not constitute cause for a procedural default. See Murray, 477 U.S. at 486; Engle, 456 U.S. at 133-34. Cause for a procedural default is not established by "[a]ttorney ignorance or inadvertence...." Coleman, 501 U.S. at 753. An error by competent counsel that does not rise to the level of ineffective assistance of counsel does not constitute cause for a procedural default. See Murray, 477 U.S. at 492; see also Jackson v. Commissioner, 227 Conn. at 135-36.

Actual prejudice, the second component of the cause and prejudice test, requires an examination of the harm stemming "from the impropriety claimed in the petition." (internal quotation marks omitted; citation omitted) Cobham v. Commissioner, 258 Conn. at 40; see also McClesky v. Zant, 499 U.S. 467, 494 (1991)("Once the petitioner has established cause, he must show "'actual prejudice" resulting from the errors of which he complains.'" (quoting United States v. Frady, 456 U.S. 152, 168 (1982))). This necessarily entails consideration of the evidence in the case, see Wainwright, 433 U.S. at 91 (substantial evidence of guilt presented at trial negated possibility of prejudice stemming from Miranda violation), and ultimately an assessment of whether the conviction remains reliable. See Murray v. Carrier, 477 U.S. at 494-95.

Cause and prejudice for a procedural default is also established where a constitutional violation has probably resulted in the conviction of an actually innocent person or where a miscarriage of justice would otherwise result. See Coleman, 501 U.S. at 748-50; Murray, 477 U.S. at 495-96; Engle, 456 U.S. at 135; Wainwright, 433 U.S. at 90-91.

The cause and prejudice test does not apply, and a procedural default is automatically overcome, when the petitioner "brings a claim alleging ineffective assistance of trial counsel." Johnson v. Commissioner, 285 Conn. 556, 571 (2008). Likewise, the cause and prejudice test does not apply, and a procedural default is automatically overcome, "when a habeas court is faced with a claim formulated within the narrow confines of ineffective assistance of appellate counsel." Johnson v. Commissioner, 285 Conn. at 569 (citing Valeriano v. Bronson, 209 Conn. 75, 76 (1988)). Rather, the test applied in each instance is the two-part

Strickland test. See Johnson, 285 Conn. at 570-72. This is because "[i]f a petitioner can prove that his attorney's performance fell below acceptable standards, and that, as a result, he was deprived of a fair trial or appeal, he will necessarily have established a basis for 'cause' and will invariably have demonstrated 'prejudice.'" Johnson, 285 Conn. at 570; see also Id. at 572.

With these principles in mind, habeas counsel must answer the defense of procedural default if it is raised in the return. The reply, see Practice Book §§ 23-31 and 23-35(c), may take one of several forms. If the habeas petition itself puts the defense in dispute or otherwise asserts cause and prejudice, habeas counsel should so indicate and need not plead anything further. See Practice Book § 23-31(a). If the habeas petition does not itself put the defense in dispute or otherwise assert cause and prejudice, habeas counsel must "allege any facts and assert any cause and prejudice claimed to permit review of any issue despite any claimed procedural default." Practice Book § 23-31(c). If the nature of the habeas claim is such that cause and prejudice is not required to overcome the defense, such as a claim of ineffective assistance of counsel at trial or on appeal, habeas counsel should so indicate. If the habeas petition reveals that a constitutional violation has probably resulted in the conviction of an innocent person, namely, the petitioner, or that a miscarriage of justice will result if the violation is not reviewed, cause and prejudice for the default is established and habeas counsel should so indicate.

G. Successive Petition

The respondent, in its return, may contend that the habeas petition constitutes a successive petition, see Practice Book § 23-29(3), in that the petition presents a ground for relief that was denied in an earlier petition. As a result, the petition should be dismissed pursuant to Practice Book §§ 23-22(2)(3), 23-29(3)(4)(5), 23-30(b), 23-34 and/or 23-37. See McClendon v. Commissioner, 93 Conn. App. 228, 231 ("[W]here successive petitions are premised on the same legal grounds and seek the same relief, the second petition will not survive a motion to dismiss unless the petition is supported by allegations and facts not reasonably available to the petitioner at the time of the original petition."), cert. denied, 277 Conn. 917 (2006). A ""ground" [is] defined as sufficient legal basis for granting the relief sought.'" McClendon v. Commissioner, 93 Conn. App. at 231(quoting Tirado v. Commissioner, 24 Conn. App. 152, 156 (1991)). If the defense of successive petition is raised in the return, habeas counsel must answer the defense in the reply. See Practice Book §§ 23-31 and 23-35(c).

When the respondent raises the successive petition defense, the habeas court need not hold an evidentiary hearing. See Negron v. Warden, 180 Conn. 153, 158 (1980); see also Carter v. Commissioner, 109 Conn. App. 300, 305-06 (2008). Instead, the habeas court can decide the issue on the pleadings. See Zollo v. Commissioner, 133 Conn. App. 266, 272, cert. granted on other grounds, 304 Conn. 910 (2012)("We agree that a motion to dismiss *may* be decided on the pleadings ... and we do not conclude that the second habeas court erred in granting the respondent's motion to dismiss on that basis." (emphasis in original; citation omitted)). "In ruling upon whether a complaint survives a motion to dismiss, [the habeas] court must take the facts to be those alleged in the complaint, including those facts necessarily implied from the allegations, construing them in a manner most favorable to the pleader...." Zollo v. Commissioner, 133 Conn. App. at 276; see generally Id. at 276-80.

Accordingly, in any case where there has been a prior habeas petition, habeas counsel must ensure that the same ground for relief is not being advanced, or, if it is being advanced, that it rests on "new facts or ... evidence not reasonably available at the time of the prior petition."

Practice Book § 23-29(3); see also Practice Book § 23-22(2)(3). Additionally, where actual innocence is a real possibility, habeas counsel must ensure that actual innocence is plead, as it will enable the petition to overcome the successive petition defense. See Schlup v. Delo, 513 U.S. 298, 316 (1995); Herrera v. Collins, 506 U.S. 390, 404 (1993). And in the reply, see Practice Book §§ 23-31 and 23-35(c), to the respondent's return, habeas counsel must emphasize the distinction between the grounds for relief, or, alternatively, the newly discovered facts or evidence that permits the ground for relief to be entertained. When actual innocence is alleged, habeas counsel must also emphasize that it would be a fundamental miscarriage of justice to dismiss the petition of a factually innocent person on the basis of the successive petition defense. See Schlup v. Delo, 513 U.S. at 316.

H. Retroactivity

The respondent, in its return, may contend that a claim in the habeas petition rests on a court decision—a new rule—that does not enjoy retroactive application. Hence, the claim should be dismissed pursuant to Practice Book §§ 23-29(5), 23-30(b), 23-34 and/or 23-37.

The test for determining whether a rule is new and, if so, whether it is applied retroactively is set forth in Teague v. Lane, 489 U.S. 288, 311-16 (1989). See Thiersaint v. Commissioner, 316 Conn. 89, 112 (2015)(Teague framework adopted for determinations under Connecticut law).

> Under *Teague*, the court "must [first] ascertain the legal landscape" as it existed at the time the petitioner's conviction became final and "ask whether the [United States] [c]onstitution, as interpreted by the precedent then existing, compels the rule.
>
> ... That is, the court must decide whether the rule is actually new." (Citation omitted; internal quotation marks omitted.) *Beard v. Banks*, 542 U.S. 406, 411 [] (2004). A constitutional rule is "new" for purposes of *Teague* "if the result was not dictated by precedent existing at the time the defendant's conviction became final." (Internal quotation marks omitted.) *Thiersaint v. Commissioner, supra*, 103.
>
> With two exceptions, a new rule will not apply retroactively to cases on collateral review. *Teague v. Lane, supra*, 489 U.S. 311-13.
>
> First, if the new rule is "substantive," that is, if the rule "places certain kinds of primary, private conduct

beyond the power of the criminal law-making authority to proscribe"; (Internal quotation marks omitted.) Thiersaint v. Commissioner, 316 Conn. 108 n.8; it must apply retroactively. "Such rules apply retroactively because they necessarily carry a significant risk that a defendant stands convicted of an act that the law does not make criminal or faces a punishment that the law cannot impose upon him." (Internal quotation marks omitted.) Schriro v. Summerlin, 542 U.S. 348, 352 [](2004).

Second, if the new rule is procedural, it applies retroactively if it is "a watershed [rule] of criminal procedure ... implicit in the concept of ordered liberty"; (citation omitted; internal question marks omitted.) Beard v. Banks, 542 U.S. 417; meaning that it "implicat[es] the fundamental fairness and accuracy of [a] criminal proceeding." (Internal quotation marks omitted.) Id.; see also Sawyer v. Smith, 497 U.S. 227, 242 [] (1990)(rule is watershed when it improves accuracy and "alter[s] our understanding of the bedrock procedural elements essential to the fairness of a proceeding" [emphasis omitted; internal quotation marks omitted]), quoting Teague v. Lane, 489 U.S. 311.

Watershed rules of criminal procedure include those that "raise the possibility that someone convicted with use of the invalidated procedure might have been acquitted otherwise." Schriro v. Summerlin, 542 U.S. 352.

The United States Supreme Court has narrowly construed this second exception and, in the twenty-five years since Teague was decided, has yet to conclued that a new rule qualifies as watershed. See Id. (class of watershed rules of criminal procedure "is extremely narrow, and it is unlikely that any ... ha[s] yet to emerge" [internal quotation marks omitted]); State v. Mares, 2014 WY 126, 335 P. 3d 487, 502 (Wyo. 2014)("[t]he [United States] Supreme Court has found no watershed rules ... since it adopted Teague" [internal quotation marks omitted]).

Casiano v. Commissioner, 317 Conn. at 62-63. In that the Teague analysis was designed to "minimiz[e] federal intrusion into state criminal proceedings[,]" state courts—including Connecticut state courts—are "free to 'apply the Teague analysis more liberally than the United States Supreme Court would otherwise apply it where a particular state interest is better served by a broader retroactivity ruling.'" (citations omitted) Casiano, 317 Conn. at 64; see Theirsaint v. Commissioner, 316 Conn. at 110 ("states are not bound by federal law when determining whether a new rule applies retroactively in a state collateral proceeding"); see also Luurtsema v. Commissioner, 299 Conn. 740, 753 n.14 (2011).

The issue of retroactivity has recently been before the Connecticut Supreme Court and United States Supreme Court. In Thiersaint v. Commissioner, supra, 316 Conn. 89, the Connecticut Supreme Court held that as a matter of Connecticut law, the United States Supreme Court's decision in Padilla v. Kentucky, 559 U.S. 356, 364-69 (2010)(adequate assistance of counsel requires that defendant be informed of the immigration consequences of the plea), is not retroactive to cases on collateral view. Thiersaint, 316 Conn. at 93, 106-24. In Casiano v. Commissioner, supra, 317 Conn. 52, the Connecticut Supreme Court held that as a matter of Connecticut law, the United States Supreme Court's decision in Miller v. Alabama, 567 U.S. ___, ___, 132 S.Ct. 2455, 2463-64, 2469 (2012)(sentencing schemes that preclude consideration of youthful age and adolescence because life imprisonment without the possibility of parole is mandatory for juvenile homicide offenders violates the 8th Amendment), is *a watershed rule of criminal procedure* that is retroactive in cases on collateral review. Casiano, 317 Conn. at 62, 61-71. Recently, in Montgomery v. Louisiana, 577 U.S. ___, No. 14-280 (Jan. 27, 2016), the United States Supreme Court held that Miller's prohibition announced *a new substantive rule* that, under the federal constitution, is retroactive in cases on state collateral review.

Other Connecticut Supreme Court cases that have considered the issue of retroactivity include State v. Payne, 303 Conn. 538, 550 n.10 (2012) (Teague retroactivity holding inapposite because new rule of law is procedural); Duperry v. Solnit, 261 Conn. 309, 322 (2002)(habeas court improperly declared and applied new constitutional rule in collateral proceeding in contravention of principle enunciated in Teague); Johnson v. Warden, 218 Conn. 791, 796-98 (1991)(habeas court improperly applied Teague retroactivity holding to new nonconstitutional rule of criminal procedure); Garcia v. Commissioner, 147 Conn. App. 669, 677 (2014)(new procedural rule not retroactive under Teague).

Accordingly, in the reply, see Practice Book §§ 23-31 and 23-35(c), habeas counsel must respond to any assertion that the decisional law the petitioner relies upon constitutes a new rule that does not enjoy retroactive application. Here, research is paramount. Habeas counsel must attempt to show either that the rule is not new (because it is dictated by existing precedent) or that one of Teague's exceptions apply. If the second exception appears applicable this should be done by explaining how the rule enhances the accuracy of convictions, by offering analogies, and by citing supportive decisions in other states. Habeas counsel also should emphasize that _Teague_ can be liberally applied as a matter of Connecticut law.

CHAPTER 21.

WITHDRAWAL OF THE HABEAS PETITION

General Statutes § 52-80 applies to habeas cases and provides that "[t]he plaintiff may withdraw any action ... before the commencement of a hearing on the merits thereof. After the commencement of a hearing on an issue of fact in any such action, the plaintiff may withdraw such action ... only by leave of the court for cause shown." Thus, a habeas petition can be withdrawn without prejudice prior to the commencement of trial. A habeas trial commences only when evidence is presented or argument on the merits is made. It does not commence just because the judge has taken the bench. See Kendall v. Commissioner, 162 Conn. App. 23 (2015).

Prior to moving under General Statutes § 52-80, habeas counsel should consider the effect the withdrawal will have on the state time limitations contained in General Statutes § 52-470(c)(d)(e)(f) and on the federal time limitation contained in Title 28, United States Code, § 2244(d)(one year clock).

CHAPTER 22.

PREPARING FOR THE HABEAS TRIAL

A. Logistics & Preparation of Exhibits

Habeas corpus trials are generally held at the Superior Court in Rockville, a location northeast of Hartford. Traveling to Rockville to testify may be difficult for lay witnesses from distant towns or other states or who have limited means. Habeas counsel must be mindful of these difficulties and should take whatever steps are necessary to ensure the attendance of such witnesses at the trial. Counsel should facilitate their attendance by providing or arranging public or private transportation. If this is a significant expenditure and habeas counsel is court-appointed, counsel should obtain authorization from the Office of Chief Public Defender to incur the expense.

To the extent possible, habeas counsel should pre-mark the petitioner's exhibits in preparation for the habeas trial. Counsel should also place the exhibits on a thumb drive, in the event the court requests that they be additionally or solely submitted in that form. A copy of the exhibits, either in paper or electronic form, should be provided to opposing counsel. An additional thumb drive should be on hand to give to the judge as a courtesy should the judge so desire.

B. Direct & Cross-Examination Outlines

Proper preparation for the habeas trial requires habeas counsel to prepare an outline of the direct examination or cross-examination of each anticipated witness. Direct examination outlines will ensure that evidence is adduced on the essential elements and alleged facts of each claim. Cross-examination outlines will ensure that information central to the outcome of the case is not omitted. <u>See, e.g.</u> <u>Antonio A. v. Commissioner</u>, 148 Conn. App. 825, 835-36 ("Our review of the transcript of the habeas trial reveals that trial counsel was not asked why he did not have a forensic psychologist or psychiatrist testify on the petitioner's behalf. He was asked only whether he had asked such a person to review the videotape of the victim's forensic interview...."), <u>cert. denied</u>, 312 Conn. 901 (2014). Overall, such outlines will ensure that in the midst of the trial, where counsel is susceptible to distraction, no important and necessary questions are omitted.

C. Subpoenas & Measures to Secure Attendance & Evidence

A witness residing in Connecticut has no legal obligation to appear at a habeas trial absent a properly issued subpoena. General Statutes §§ 1-3b, 52-143 and 52-144 empower habeas counsel to issue subpoenas and to seek court intervention if the subpoenas are ignored. If the witness resides out of state, it may be difficult to secure the attendance of the witness. The uniform act to secure the attendance of out-of-state witnesses, <u>see</u> General Statutes § 54-82i(c), is of no benefit because the habeas proceeding is a civil proceeding. The best course of action may simply be to offer to compensate the witness for his or her travel costs or to provide the transportation by buying a plane or bus ticket or sending a livery service. Because the cost of these measures may exceed that which is permitted in the subpoena statutes, habeas court approval should first be obtained. An alternative course of action may be to move the habeas court for permission to depose the witness and to introduce the transcript at the habeas trial. <u>See</u> Practice Book § 23-39.

If the witness is incarcerated in a Connecticut correctional facility, habeas counsel should contact the habeas court clerk's office to facilitate the attendance of the witness at the habeas trial pursuant to General Statutes § 18-81a. Witnesses incarcerated in other states or in federal correctional facilities are very difficult to secure, particularly when officials learn that the habeas proceeding is a civil proceeding. Habeas counsel is advised to contact the facility warden to learn the applicable policies and procedures. A practical solution may be to secure the inmate's testimony by an interactive audiovisual devise under Practice Book §§ 23-40(b) and 23-68.

If hospital records are needed for the habeas trial, General Statutes § 4-104 permits habeas counsel to subpoena the records under seal to the Clerk's Office. However, opening, reviewing and introducing the hospital records cannot occur without the authorization of the habeas court and the subject of the records. <u>See</u> Practice Book §§ 7-18 and 15-4.

In that a habeas proceeding is a civil action, the signed report of the petitioner's treating physician or mental health professional is admissible in evidence without the provider taking the witness stand. See General Statutes § 52-174(b). Before trial, however, habeas counsel should give notice under Practice Book §§ 13-4 and 23-38 that the petitioner intends to invoke the statute.

D. Preparing the Client to Testify

If the petitioner's testimony is needed to prove one or more of the habeas claims, the petitioner must be prepared to testify. Many clients will not have testified at the original criminal trial or experienced giving testimony under oath. Further, responding to questions posed by a lawyer takes the kind of discipline that normally is not exercised in the petitioner's everyday life. Thus, it is imperative that habeas counsel get the petitioner ready to testify to the facts needed to establish the claims in the petition and to field questions on cross-examination. Counsel should review with the petitioner the areas or subjects that will be covered on direct examination, including some of the specific questions that will be asked. Counsel should also ensure that the petitioner's memory of events, including his or her interaction with trial or appellate counsel, is sufficiently refreshed. Habeas counsel should also review with the petitioner the reasonably anticipated questions on cross-examination and the need for the petitioner to keep his answers short and on point. Counsel should also explain to the petitioner that when an objection is made, the question should not be answered, if at all, until the court makes a ruling.

Related to the testimony of the petitioner at the habeas trial are two issues. First, if the petitioner's testimony will pertain to only some of the habeas claims, then a ruling must be obtained, preventing the respondent, on cross-examination, from delving into the other claims. This can be done in advance of the testimony, see Practice Book §§ 15-3 and 42-15, or during the testimony with a "beyond the scope" objection. Second, and arguably more important, a ruling should be obtained in advance of the testimony that the respondent is precluded from examining the petitioner on the historical facts of crime, as this will infringe on the petitioner's constitutional and statutory right to remain silent and to due process of law at any retrial. Here, the protective order provisions contained in Practice Book §§ 13-5 and 40-40, et seq., should be utilized.

CHAPTER 23.

HABEAS TRIAL

A. Evidence

The petitioner has the right under Article First, § 12 of the Connecticut Constitution and General Statutes § 52-470(a) to have the habeas court hear the testimony and arguments related to the claims contained in the petition. See General Statutes § 52-470(a)("The court or judge hearing any habeas shall proceed in a summary way to determine the facts and issues in the case, *by hearing the testimony and arguments in the case*...." (emphasis added)). In <u>Mercer v. Commissioner</u>, 230 Conn. 88 (1994), the Connecticut Supreme Court re-affirmed that "absent an explicit exception, an evidentiary hearing is always required before a habeas petition may be dismissed." <u>Mercer</u>, 230 Conn. at 93. Under the case law, the only recognized exception is that contained in Practice Book §

23-29—where the petitioner brought a previous habeas petition and the current petition fails "'to state[] new facts or proffer[] new evidence not reasonably available at the previous hearing.'" Id. (quoting Negron v. Warden, 180 Conn. 153, 158 (1980)); but see Practice Book § 23-24 *Habeas Corpus—Preliminary Consideration of Judicial Authority* and § 23-37 *Habeas Corpus—Summary Judgment.*

The petitioner bears the burden of proof at the trial, and the standard of proof is a fair preponderance of the evidence. See Gaines v. Commissioner, 306 Conn. 664, 666 (2012).

At any stage of the trial, if there is a material variance between the amended petition and the proof, habeas counsel should request permission to amend the petition, citing Practice Book § 10-62. See Zollo v. Commissioner, 133 Conn. App. 266, 280 (noting the petitioner's failure to utilize the remedy of requesting permission to amend the petition to conform to the proof under Practice Book § 10-62), cert. granted on other grounds, 304 Conn. 910 (2012); Reddick v. Commissioner, 51 Conn. App. 474, 476 (1999)(petitioner received permission to amend petition to conform to proof at hearing).

If, at the close of the petitioner's case-in-chief, the petitioner has failed to make out a prima facie case, the respondent can move to dismiss the petition under Practice Book §§ 15-8 and 23-29(5). See McMillion v. Commissioner, 151 Conn. App. 861, 862-81 (2014). "A prima facie case ... is one sufficient to raise an issue to go to the trier of fact.... In order to establish a prima facie case, the proponent must submit evidence which, if credited, is sufficient to establish the facts or facts which it is adduced to prove." Id. at 870. "At the time a court is considering a motion for dismissal for failure to make out a prima facie case, a petitioner is not required to overcome any of the respondent's defenses. Although a determination of the truthfulness of a statement is a question of fact for the trier, a trial court would act improperly [if] it made findings of fact at this stage instead of taking the plaintiff's evidence ... as true." (internal quotation marks omitted; citation omitted) Id. at 880.

When the petition alleges ineffective assistance of counsel, the petitioner is under no legal obligation to call counsel as a witness at the habeas trial. Cf. D'Amico v. Warden, 193 Conn. 144, 153 (1984)("We have serious reservations as to whether ... an [adverse] inference can be justified, because an attorney, whose competence is implicitly under attack in a habeas corpus proceeding ... is hardly a witness whom a disgruntled client would 'naturally' have produced.").

B. Closing Argument

Closing argument at the conclusion of the habeas trial is not often invited by the judge, but habeas counsel should nevertheless be prepared to succinctly summarize the evidence of counsel's deficiencies, the prejudice that ensued, and the appropriate remedy.

C. Post-Trial Brief

The post-trial brief, if requested or permitted by the habeas court, should also summarize the evidence adduced in support of the claimed deficiencies and the attendant prejudice, but in far greater detail than a closing argument. Each argument should also be supported by ample legal authority. The pertinent pages of the habeas trial transcript should also be cited. In that it may take several weeks or months for the court reporter to prepare the transcript, habeas counsel should request that the due date of the brief be extended to 30 or 45 days after receipt of the transcript.

Habeas counsel should also be prepared to submit proposed findings of fact should the court so request. Here again, the habeas trial transcript will be needed.

CHAPTER 24.
HABEAS DECISION

General Statutes § 52-470(a) states that "[t]he court or judge hearing any habeas corpus shall proceed in a summary way to determine the facts and issues of the case, by hearing the testimony and arguments in the case, and shall inquire fully into the cause of imprisonment and thereupon dispose of the case as law and justice require." See James L. v. Commissioner, 245 Conn. 132, 148 (1998)("A habeas court must fashion a remedy appropriate to the constitutional right it seeks to vindicate."); Gaines v. Manson, 194 Conn. 510, 516 (1984)("In the adjudication of petitions for habeas corpus, the remedies available to a court depend upon the constitutional rights that are being vindicated."); see also Practice Book § 23-34 *Habeas Corpus—Summary Procedures for Habeas Corpus Petitions* and § 23-37 *Habeas Corpus—Summary Judgment*.

The habeas court must "render judgment not later than one hundred and twenty days from the completion date of the trial...." General Statutes § 51-183b. However, "[t]he parties may waive the provisions of this section." Id.; see also Foote v. Commissioner, 125 Conn. App. 296 (2010). If the judgment is rendered beyond the 120-day statutory deadline and the parties have not waived the deadline or consented to the late filing, the petitioner can move to set aside the judgment, seeking a new habeas trial as a remedy. See Foote v. Commissioner, 125 Conn. App. at 297-98, 307.

The habeas court has the authority, under General Statutes § 52-493, to issue any interlocutory or final order that may appear to be an appropriate form of relief for the claims raised in the petition.

CHAPTER 25.

HABEAS APPEAL

The petitioner has a qualified right to appeal an adverse decision on the habeas petition. General Statutes § 52-470(g) states: "No appeal from the judgment rendered in a habeas corpus proceeding brought by or on behalf of a person who has been convicted of a crime in order to obtain such person's release may be taken unless the appellant, within ten days after the case is decided, petitions the judge before who the case was tried or, if such judge is unavailable, a judge of the Superior Court designated by the Chief Clerk Administrator, to certify that a question is involved in the decision which ought to be reviewed by the court having jurisdiction and the judge so certifies." See also Practice Book § 80-1 (petition for certification must be filed within ten days after habeas case is decided).

The appeal must be filed "within twenty days from the issuance of the notice of decision on the petition for certification, unless an application for waiver of fees, costs and security is filed pursuant to § 63-6, in which event the appeal shall be filed within twenty days from the decision on the application." Practice Book § 80-1. The appeal is governed by Practice Book §§ 60-5 and 61-1, et seq. to 80-1, et seq.

If the habeas court denies the petition for certification, the petitioner must establish on appeal, as a threshold matter, that the denial was an abuse of discretion. See Simms v. Warden, 229 Conn. 178, 186-87 (1994)(Simms I). This is done by demonstrating on appeal "'that the issues are debatable among jurists of reason; that a court could resolve the issues [in a different manner]; or that the questions are adequate to deserve encouragement to proceed further.'" Simms v. Warden, 230 Conn. 608, 616 (1994)(Simms II)(quoting Lozada v. Deeds, 498 U.S. 430, 432 (1991)); see Castonguay v. Commissioner, 300 Conn. 649, 657-58 (2011)(same). This necessarily requires the Connecticut Appellate Court or Connecticut Supreme Court, as the case may be, to "'consider the merits of the petitioner's underlying claims to determine whether the habeas court reasonably determined that the petitioner's appeal was frivolous.'" Castonguay v. Commissioner, 300

Conn. at 658 (quoting Taylor v. Commissioner, 284 Conn. 433, 449 (2007)); see also Paulino v. Commissioner, 155 Conn. App. 154, 159-60, cert. denied, 317 Conn. 912 (2015).

A. Standard of Review—Dismissal Based on Defense

The following standard of review is employed when a habeas petition has been dismissed based on a defense: "The conclusions reached by the trial court in its decision to dismiss [a] habeas petition are matters of law, subject to plenary review.... [W]hen the legal conclusions of the court are challenged, [the appeals court] must determine whether they are legally and logically correct ... and whether they find support in the facts that appear in the record." (internal quotation marks omitted; citation omitted) Johnson v. Commissioner, 285 Conn. 556, 566 (2008); see Paulino v. Commissioner, 155 Conn. App. 154, 160, cert. denied, 317 Conn. 912 (2015); Thorpe v. Commissioner, 73 Conn. App. 773, 776-77 (2002).

B. Standard of Review—Denial on the

Merits

The following standard of review is employed when a habeas petition has been rejected on the merits: "The habeas court is afforded broad discretion in making its factual findings, and those findings will not be disturbed unless they are clearly erroneous.... Historical facts constitute a recital of external events and the credibility of their narrators.... Accordingly, [t]he habeas judge, as the trier of facts, is the sole arbiter of the credibility of witnesses and the weight to be given to their testimony.... The application of the habeas court's factual findings to the pertinent legal standard, however, presents a mixed question of law and fact, which is subject to plenary review." (internal quotation marks omitted; citations omitted) Gaines v. Commissioner, 306 Conn. 664, 677 (2012); see also Jackson v. Commissioner, 149 Conn. App. 681, 690 (appeals court will exercise plenary review on the issue of "whether the facts found by the habeas court constitute[] a violation of the petitioner's constitutional right to effective assistance of counsel"), cert. granted on other grounds, 313 Conn. 901 (2014); Id. at 711 ("This court does not retry the case or evaluate the credibility of witnesses. Rather, we must defer to the [trier of fact's] assessment of the credibility of the witnesses based on its firsthand observation of their conduct, demeanor and attitude." (internal quotation marks omitted; citation omitted)).

As to the claims raised on appeal, the Connecticut Appellate Court or the Connecticut Supreme Court "will not consider claims not raised in the habeas petition or decided by the habeas court. ... Appellate review of claims not raised before the habeas court would amount to an ambuscade of the [habeas] judge." (internal quotation marks omitted; citation omitted) Jackson, 149 Conn. App. at 687-88.

CHAPTER 26.
CONCLUSION

"It must never be forgotten that the writ of habeas corpus is the precious safeguard of personal liberty and there is no higher duty than to maintain it unimpaired."

Bowen v. Johnston, 306 U.S. 19, 26 (1939)

www.ingramcontent.com/pod-product-compliance
Lightning Source LLC
Chambersburg PA
CBHW070525200326
41519CB00013B/2930